决战决胜

中国脱贫攻坚的伟大实践

SECURING A FINAL VICTORY
China's Poverty Reduction Practice

新　华　通　讯　社
原国务院扶贫开发领导小组办公室　编

新 华 出 版 社
XINHUA PUBLISHING HOUSE

　　2021年7月1日，庆祝中国共产党成立100周年大会在北京天安门广场隆重举行。中共中央总书记、国家主席、中央军委主席习近平发表重要讲话。（新华社记者鞠鹏摄）

Chinese President Xi Jinping, also general secretary of the CPC Central Committee and chairman of the CMC, delivers an important speech at a ceremony marking the 100th anniversary of the founding of the CPC at Tiananmen Square in Beijing, capital of China, July 1, 2021. (Xinhua/Ju Peng)

经过全党全国各族人民共同努力，在迎来中国共产党成立一百周年的重要时刻，我国脱贫攻坚战取得了全面胜利，现行标准下9899万农村贫困人口全部脱贫，832个贫困县全部摘帽，12.8万个贫困村全部出列，区域性整体贫困得到解决，完成了消除绝对贫困的艰巨任务，创造了又一个彪炳史册的人间奇迹！这是中国人民的伟大光荣，是中国共产党的伟大光荣，是中华民族的伟大光荣！

——2021年2月25日，习近平在全国脱贫攻坚总结表彰大会上的讲话

Through the joint efforts of the whole Party and the people of all ethnic groups, at the important moment of the centenary of the founding of the Communist Party of China, China has won a complete victory in the fight against poverty. Under the current standard, 98.99 million rural poor people have all been lifted out of poverty. All 832 poverty-stricken counties and 128,000 poverty-stricken villages have shaken off poverty. The overall regional poverty has been solved, and the arduous task of eliminating absolute poverty has been completed, creating another miracle in the of history of mankind! This is the great glory of the Chinese people, the Communist Party of China and the Chinese nation!

—From Chinese President Xi Jinping's speech at a grand gathering to mark the nation's poverty alleviation accomplishments and honor model poverty fighters on Feb.25, 2021.

目 录

CONTENTS

关怀·足迹

CARING & FOOTPRINT

消除贫困、改善民生、实现共同富裕，是社会主义的本质要求，是我们党的重要使命。

——2015 年 6 月 18 日，习近平在部分省区市党委主要负责同志座谈会上的讲话

40 多年来，我先后在中国县、市、省、中央工作，扶贫始终是我工作的一个重要内容，我花的精力最多。

——2015 年 10 月 16 日，习近平在 2015 减贫与发展高层论坛上的主旨演讲

It is an essential requirement of socialism as well as a key mission of the CPC to eradicate poverty, improve people's livelihood and achieve common prosperity.

—President Xi Jinping said at a symposium attended by Party chiefs of some provincial-level regions on June 18, 2015.

Over the past more than 40 years, I have worked at the county, city, provincial and central levels in China. Poverty alleviation has always been an important part of my work, to which I have devoted most of my energy.

—President Xi Jinping said when addressing the Global Poverty Reduction and Development Forum on Oct. 16, 2015.

　　2022 年 10 月 27 日，中共中央总书记、国家主席、中央军委主席习近平带领中共中央政治局常委李强、赵乐际、王沪宁、蔡奇、丁薛祥、李希，瞻仰延安革命纪念地。这是习近平等在延安革命纪念馆，参观《伟大历程——中共中央在延安十三年历史陈列》。（新华社记者王晔摄）

Xi Jinping visits an exhibition on the 13 years of the Communist Party of China (CPC) Central Committee in Yan'an at the Yan'an Revolutionary Memorial Hall in Yan'an, northwest China's Shaanxi Province, Oct. 27, 2022. Xi Jinping, general secretary of the CPC Central Committee, led members of the Standing Committee of the CPC Central Committee Political Bureau on Thursday to visit Yan'an, an old revolutionary base in northwest China's Shaanxi Province. Xi, also Chinese president and chairman of the Central Military Commission, was accompanied by Li Qiang, Zhao Leji, Wang Huning, Cai Qi, Ding Xuexiang and Li Xi. (Xinhua/Wang Ye)

2021 年 2 月 25 日，全国脱贫攻坚总结表彰大会在北京人民大会堂隆重举行。习近平、李克强、栗战书、汪洋、王沪宁、赵乐际、韩正、王岐山等出席大会。（新华社记者鞠鹏摄）

Xi Jinping, Li Keqiang, Li Zhanshu, Wang Yang, Wang Huning, Zhao Leji, Han Zheng and Wang Qishan attend a grand gathering to mark the nation's poverty alleviation accomplishments and honor model poverty fighters at the Great Hall of the People in Beijing, capital of China, Feb. 25, 2021. (Xinhua/Ju Peng)

2012 年，党的十八大提出全面建成小康社会奋斗目标，十八大召开后不久，习近平总书记就指出"小康不小康，关键看老乡，关键在贫困的老乡能不能脱贫"，强调"决不能落下一个贫困地区、一个贫困群众"，拉开了新时代脱贫攻坚的序幕。图为 2012 年 11 月 15 日，在党的十八届一中全会上当选的中共中央总书记习近平和中央政治局常委李克强、张德江、俞正声、刘云山、王岐山、张高丽在北京人民大会堂同采访十八大的中外记者见面。（新华社记者谢环驰摄）

In 2012, the 18th CPC National Congress set the goal of building a moderately prosperous society in all respects. Soon after that, Xi enunciated, "To achieve initial prosperity in the countryside, it is essential to raise rural living standards and particularly those of impoverished villagers", launching the campaign against poverty in the new era. He also stressed, "No single poor area or single poor person should be left behind in achieving this goal". Xi Jinping, General Secretary of the CPC Central Committee elected at the First Plenary Session of the 18th CPC Central Committee, and members of the Standing Committee of the Political Bureau of the Central Committee, including Li Keqiang, Zhang Dejiang, Yu Zhengsheng, Liu Yunshan, Wang Qishan and Zhang Gaoli, meet with Chinese and foreign journalists covering the 18th CPC National Congress at the Great Hall of the People in Beijing, November 15, 2012.(Xinhua/Xie Huanchi)

2021 年 2 月 25 日，全国脱贫攻坚总结表彰大会在北京人民大会堂隆重举行。中共中央总书记、国家主席、中央军委主席习近平在大会上发表重要讲话。（新华社记者李学仁摄）

Chinese President Xi Jinping, also general secretary of the Communist Party of China Central Committee and chairman of the Central Military Commission, delivers an important speech at a grand gathering to mark the nation's poverty alleviation accomplishments and honor model poverty fighters at the Great Hall of the People in Beijing, capital of China, Feb. 25, 2021. (Xinhua/Li Xueren)

　　2021 年 2 月 25 日，全国脱贫攻坚总结表彰大会在北京人民大会堂隆重举行。会前，习近平等会见全国脱贫攻坚楷模荣誉称号获得者，全国脱贫攻坚先进个人、先进集体代表，全国脱贫攻坚楷模荣誉称号个人获得者和因公牺牲全国脱贫攻坚先进个人亲属代表等。（新华社记者谢环驰摄）

Chinese President Xi Jinping, also general secretary of the Communist Party of China Central Committee and chairman of the Central Military Commission, meets with role models in China's poverty alleviation fight and relatives of those model poverty fighters who lost their lives in the country's anti-poverty cause before a grand gathering to mark the nation's poverty alleviation accomplishments and honor model poverty fighters at the Great Hall of the People in Beijing, capital of China, Feb. 25, 2021. (Xinhua/Xie Huanchi)

　　2021 年 2 月 25 日，全国脱贫攻坚总结表彰大会在北京人民大会堂隆重举行。（新华社记者殷博古摄）

A grand gathering is held to mark the nation's poverty alleviation accomplishments and honor model poverty fighters at the Great Hall of the People in Beijing, capital of China, Feb. 25, 2021. (Xinhua/Yin Bogu)

　　2020 年 3 月 6 日，中共中央总书记、国家主席、中央军委主席习近平在北京出席决战决胜脱贫攻坚座谈会并发表重要讲话。2015 年以来，中央就打赢脱贫攻坚战召开了 7 个专题会议。2015 年在延安召开陕甘宁革命老区脱贫致富座谈会、在贵阳召开部分省区市扶贫攻坚与"十三五"时期经济社会发展座谈会，2016 年在银川召开东西部扶贫协作座谈会，2017 年在太原召开深度贫困地区脱贫攻坚座谈会，2018 年在成都召开打好精准脱贫攻坚战座谈会，2019 年在重庆召开解决"两不愁三保障"突出问题座谈会。（新华社记者鞠鹏摄）

President Xi Jinping, also general secretary of the Communist Party of China (CPC) Central Committee and chairman of the Central Military Commission (CMC), attends a symposium on securing a decisive victory in poverty eradication in Beijing on March 6, 2020 and delivers an important speech. The CPC Central Committee has held seven special symposiums on winning the battle against poverty since 2015. In 2015, a symposium on poverty eradication in old revolutionary base areas was held in Yan'an City, northwest China's Shaanxi Province. In 2016, a symposium on collaboration on poverty alleviation between the eastern and western regions was held in Yinchuan. In 2017, a symposium on poverty eradication in areas of extreme poverty was held in Taiyuan. In 2018, a symposium on targeted poverty eradication was held in Chengdu. In 2019, a symposium on resolving prominent problems concerning the basic living needs of poor populations and their access to compulsory education, basic medical services, and safe housing was held in Chongqing. (Xinhua/Ju Peng)

2012 年 12 月 29 日至 30 日，中共中央总书记、中共中央军委主席习近平在河北省阜平县看望慰问困难群众。图为 30 日，习近平在龙泉关镇顾家台村的小卖部，了解农村日常用品供应情况。（新华社记者兰红光摄）

Xi Jinping, general secretary of the CPC Central Committee and chairman of the CMC, visits a grocery in the Gujiatai Village of Longquanguan Township, Fuping County, north China's Hebei Province, Dec. 30, 2012. Xi inspected Fuping County from Dec. 29 to 30, 2012. (Xinhua/Lan Hongguang)

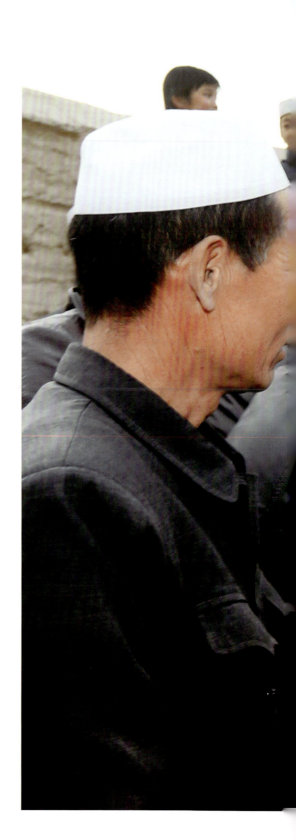

2013 年 2 月 3 日，中共中央总书记、中共中央军委主席习近平沿着陡峭山路来到甘肃省东乡族自治县布楞沟村看望东乡族群众。图为习近平和村民们热情握手。（新华社记者兰红光摄）

Xi Jinping, general secretary of the CPC Central Committee and chairman of the CMC, shakes hands with villagers in Bulenggou Village of Dongxiang Autonomous County, northwest China's Gansu Province, Feb. 3, 2013. Xi came to the village along the steep mountain road to visit residents of the Dongxiang ethnic group. (Xinhua/Lan Hongguang)

　　2013 年 11 月 3 日至 5 日，中共中央总书记、国家主席、中央军委主席习近平在湖南考察。图为 3 日下午，习近平在湖南省花垣县排碧乡十八洞村同村干部和村民座谈。（新华社记者王晔摄）

President Xi Jinping, also general secretary of the CPC Central Committee and chairman of the CMC, talks with local villagers and cadres in Shibadong Village in Paibi Township of Huayuan County in the Tujia-Miao Autonomous Prefecture of Xiangxi, central China's Hunan Province, Nov. 3, 2013. Xi took an inspection tour to Hunan Province from Nov. 3 to 5. (Xinhua/Wang Ye)

2013 年 11 月 3 日至 5 日，中共中央总书记、国家主席、中央军委主席习近平在湖南考察。图为 3 日下午，习近平在湘西土家族苗族自治州花垣县排碧乡十八洞村苗族村民施齐文家中同一家人促膝交谈。（新华社记者兰红光摄）

President Xi Jinping, also general secretary of the CPC Central Committee and chairman of the CMC, talks with family members of Shi Qiwen, a villager in Shibadong Village in Paibi Township of Huayuan County in the Tujia-Miao Autonomous Prefecture of Xiangxi, central China's Hunan Province, Nov. 3, 2013. Xi took an inspection tour to Hunan Province from Nov. 3 to 5. (Xinhua/Lan Hongguang)

2013 年 11 月 3 日至 5 日，中共中央总书记、国家主席、中央军委主席习近平在湖南考察。图为 3 日下午，习近平来到湘西土家族苗族自治州凤凰县廖家桥镇菖蒲塘村了解扶贫开发和水果产业发展情况。（新华社记者兰红光摄）

Chinese President Xi Jinping, also general secretary of the Communist Party of China (CPC) Central Committee and chairman of Central Military Commission, gives way to villagers at Changputang Village of Liaojiaqiao Township in Fenghuang County of the Tujia-Miao Autonomous Prefecture of Xiangxi, central China's Hunan Province, Nov. 3, 2013. Xi took an inspection tour to Hunan Province from Nov. 3 to Nov. 5. (Xinhua/Lan Hongguang)

　　2014年3月17日至18日，中共中央总书记、国家主席、中央军委主席习近平在河南省兰考县调研指导党的群众路线教育实践活动。图为3月17日，习近平在东坝头乡张庄村看望困难户85岁老人张景枝。（新华社记者李学仁摄）

President Xi Jinping, also general secretary of the CPC Central Committee and chairman of the CMC, visits Zhang Jingzhi, an 85-year-old villager, at Zhangzhuang Village, Lankao County in central China's Henan Province, March 17, 2014. Xi made an inspection tour in Lankao from March 17 to 18, directing the "mass line" educational campaign that was initiated by the CPC in June 2013 to bring the Party closer to the people. (Xinhua/Li Xueren)

2014 年 4 月 27 日至 30 日，中共中央总书记、国家主席、中央军委主席习近平在新疆考察。图为 28 日下午，习近平在新疆果业集团有限公司了解果品加工、包装、配送等情况。（新华社记者兰红光摄）

Chinese President Xi Jinping, also general secretary of the CPC Central Committee and chairman of the CMC, visits a major fruit company in northwest China's Xinjiang Uygur Autonomous Region, April 28, 2014. Xi had an inspection tour in Xinjiang from April 27 to 30, 2014. (Xinhua/Lan Hongguang)

2015 年 2 月 13 日至 16 日，中共中央总书记、国家主席、中央军委主席习近平来到陕西，看望慰问广大干部群众，向全国各族人民致以新春祝福，祝伟大祖国繁荣昌盛、各族人民幸福安康。图为 13 日上午，习近平在延川县文安驿镇梁家河村调研时同村民边走边聊。（新华社记者兰红光摄）

President Xi Jinping, also general secretary of the CPC Central Committee and chairman of the CMC, walks and has a conversation with local people during an inspection tour at Liangjiahe Village, Wen'anyi Township of Yanchuan County in northwest China's Shaanxi Province, Feb. 13, 2015, during his tour in Shaanxi from Feb. 13 to 16 of 2015 to extend festival greetings to locals and people across the nation ahead of the Spring Festival. (Xinhua/Lan Hongguang)

2015 年 2 月 13 日上午，中共中央总书记、国家主席、中央军委主席习近平在延安市延川县文安驿镇梁家河村察看自己当年住过的知青窑洞。（新华社记者兰红光摄）

President Xi Jinping, also general secretary of the CPC Central Committee and chairman of the CMC, visits a cave dwelling he lived in during his teenage when he came to Liangjiahe Village as part of a campaign launched by Chairman Mao Zedong that asked urban youth to experience rural life, in Wen'anyi Township of Yanchuan County, Yan'an, northwest China's Shaanxi Province, Feb. 13, 2015. (Xinhua/Lan Hongguang)

　　2016 年 4 月 24 日至 27 日，中共中央总书记、国家主席、中央军委主席习近平在安徽调研。图为 24 日下午，习近平在金寨县花石乡大湾村村民汪能保家中察看扶贫手册。（新华社记者李涛摄）

Presient Xi Jinping, also general secretary of the CPC Central Committee and chairman of the CMC, checks a workbook on poverty alleviation while visiting a villager's home at Dawan Village of Huashi Township in Jinzhai County, east China's Anhui Province on April 24, 2016. Xi made an inspection tour in Anhui from April 24 to 27 of 2016. (Xinhua/Li Tao)

　　2016 年 7 月 18 日至 20 日，中共中央总书记、国家主席、中央军委主席习近平在宁夏调研考察。图为 19 日上午，习近平在银川市永宁县闽宁镇原隆移民村回族移民群众海国宝家中看望。（新华社记者李涛摄）

President Xi Jinping, also general secretary of the CPC Central Committee and chairman of the CMC, visits villager of Hui ethnic group Hai Guobao's home in the Yuanlong Migrant Village of Minning Town in Yinchuan, capital of northwest China's Ningxia Hui Autonomous Region, July 19, 2016. Xi made a three-day inspection tour in Ningxia.(Xinhua/Li Tao)

2018年4月11日至13日，中共中央总书记、国家主席、中央军委主席习近平在海南考察。图为13日上午，习近平在海口市秀英区石山镇施茶村考察时，同村民亲切握手。（新华社记者谢环驰摄）

Presient Xi Jinping, also general secretary of the CPC Central Committee and chairman of the CMC, shakes hands with villagers in Shicha Village in Shishan Township of Xiuying District in Haikou City, south China's Hainan Province, during his inspection tour from April 11 to 13, 2018. (Xinhua/Xie Huanchi)

2018年4月24日至28日，中共中央总书记、国家主席、中央军委主席习近平在湖北考察。图为24日下午，习近平在宜昌市许家冲村与村民亲切交谈。（新华社记者鞠鹏摄）

Chinese President Xi Jinping, also general secretary of the CPC Central Committee and chairman of the CMC, talks with residents at Xujiachong Village of Taipingxi Town in Yichang City, central China's Hubei Province, April 24, 2018. (Xinhua/Ju Peng)

　　2018年9月25日至28日，中共中央总书记、国家主席、中央军委主席习近平在东北三省考察，主持召开深入推进东北振兴座谈会。图为25日，习近平在七星农场万亩大地号与农场工人们亲切交谈。（新华社记者谢环驰摄）

Chinese President Xi Jinping, also general secretary of the CPC Central Committee and chairman of the CMC, talks with workers at Qixing farm, northeast China's Heilongjiang Province, Sept. 25, 2018. Xi inspected the northeastern provinces of Heilongjiang, Jilin and Liaoning from Sept. 25 to 28, 2018. (Xinhua/Xie Huanchi)

　　2018 年 9 月 28 日，中共中央总书记、国家主席、中央军委主席习近平在辽宁考察。图为习近平来到东华园社区，实地考察抚顺市采煤沉陷区避险搬迁安置情况。（新华社记者鞠鹏摄）

Chinese President Xi Jinping, also general secretary of the CPC Central Committee and chairman of the CMC, visits Donghuayuan, a resettlement community for residents from coal-mining area in Fushun, northeast China's Liaoning Province, Sept. 28, 2018. (Xinhua/Ju Peng)

　　2019 年 4 月 15 日，中共中央总书记、国家主席、中央军委主席习近平在重庆考察调研。图为在石柱土家族自治县中益乡华溪村，习近平徒步前往农户家中，实地了解脱贫攻坚工作进展和解决"两不愁三保障"突出问题情况。（新华社记者谢环驰摄）

Presient Xi Jinping, also general secretary of the CPC Central Committee and chairman of the CMC, walks to a villager's home to learn about the progress of poverty alleviation and in solving prominent problems, including meeting the basic need of food and clothing and guaranteeing compulsory education, basic medical care and safe housing, in Huaxi Village of Shizhu Tujia Autonomous County, southwest China's Chongqing Municipality, April 15, 2019. (Xinhua/Xie Huanchi)

　　2019年5月20日，中共中央总书记、国家主席、中央军委主席习近平在江西省赣州市于都县梓山镇潭头村看望当地群众，同乡亲们亲切握手。（新华社记者鞠鹏摄）

Presient Xi Jinping, also general secretary of the CPC Central Committee and chairman of the CMC, visits and shakes hands with residents of Tantou Village in Yudu County, Ganzhou City, east China's Jiangxi Province, May 20, 2019. (Xinhua/Ju Peng)

2019 年 7 月 15 日至 16 日，中共中央总书记、国家主席、中央军委主席习近平在内蒙古考察并指导开展"不忘初心、牢记使命"主题教育。图为 15 日下午，习近平在赤峰市喀喇沁旗河南街道马鞍山村村民张国利家，同基层干部群众代表亲切交流。（新华社记者谢环驰摄）

Chinese President Xi Jinping, also general secretary of the CPC Central Committee and chairman of the CMC, visits Maanshan Village in Harqin Banner, Chifeng City, China's Inner Mongolia Autonomous Region, July 15, 2019. Xi made an inspection tour in Inner Mongolia from July 15 to 16, 2019. (Xinhua/Xie Huanchi)

2019年9月17日上午，正在河南考察调研的中共中央总书记、国家主席、中央军委主席习近平来到光山县文殊乡东岳村考察当地脱贫攻坚工作成效和中办在光山县扶贫工作情况。（新华社记者谢环驰摄）

President Xi Jinping, also general secretary of the CPC Central Committee and chairman of the CMC, inspects local poverty alleviation work at Dongyue Village, Guangshan County, as well as the poverty reduction work by the General Office of CPC Central Committee in the county, during his inspection tour in central China's Henan Province on Sept. 17, 2019. (Xinhua/Xie Huanchi)

　　中共中央总书记、国家主席、中央军委主席习近平赴云南考察，看望慰问基层干部群众。图为 2020 年 1 月 19 日下午，习近平来到腾冲市清水乡三家村中寨司莫拉佤族村，向大家送上新春祝福。（新华社记者鞠鹏摄）

Presient Xi Jinping, also general secretary of the CPC Central Committee and chairman of the CMC, visits a village of the Wa ethnic group to extend his Chinese New Year's greetings to the villagers in Qingshui Township in Tengchong City, southwest China's Yunnan Province, Jan. 19, 2020. (Xinhua/Ju Peng)

2020 年 4 月 21 日，中共中央总书记、国家主席、中央军委主席习近平来到陕西省安康市平利县老县镇，在茶园考察脱贫攻坚情况。（新华社记者燕雁摄）

Presient Xi Jinping, also general secretary of the CPC Central Committee and chairman of the CMC, inspects poverty alleviation work in a tea farm of Laoxian Township, Pingli County in Ankang City, northwest China's Shaanxi Province, April 21, 2020. (Xinhua/Yan Yan)

　　2020 年 5 月 11 日，中共中央总书记、国家主席、中央军委主席习近平赴山西考察调研。这是习近平在大同市云州区有机黄花标准化种植基地了解巩固脱贫攻坚成果工作情况。（新华社记者李学仁摄）

Presient Xi Jinping, also general secretary of the CPC Central Committee and chairman of the CMC, learns about poverty alleviation efforts in an organic daylily farm in Yunzhou District of Datong City, north China's Shanxi Province, May 11, 2020. (Xinhua/Li Xueren)

2020 年 5 月 11 日下午，习近平在大同市云州区西坪镇坊城新村，关心询问搬迁户白高山一家人的生产生活状况。（新华社记者谢环驰摄）

Chinese President Xi Jinping, general secretary of the Communist Party of China Central Committee and chairman of the Central Military Commission, chats with local villagers in Xiping Township in Datong City, north China's Shanxi Province, May 11, 2020. (Xinhua/Xie Huanchi)

2020 年 6 月 8 日下午，中共中央总书记、国家主席、中央军委主席习近平在吴忠市红寺堡区红寺堡镇弘德村看望移民搬迁群众，向村民们挥手致意。（新华社记者谢环驰摄）

Chinese President Xi Jinping, also general secretary of the CPC Central Committee and chairman of the CMC, waves at villagers as he visits Hongde Village in Wuzhong City, northwest China's Ningxia Hui Autonomous Region, June 8, 2020. (Xinhua/Xie Huanchi)

　　2020 年 7 月 22 日至 24 日，中共中央总书记、国家主席、中央军委主席习近平在吉林省考察。图为 7 月 22 日下午，习近平考察四平市梨树县国家百万亩绿色食品原料（玉米）标准化生产基地核心示范区地块。（新华社记者鞠鹏摄）

Chinese President Xi Jinping, also general secretary of the CPC Central Committee and chairman of the CMC, learns about grain production, the protection and use of black soil at a demonstration zone for green food production in Lishu County of Siping City, northeast China's Jilin Province, July 22, 2020. Xi Jinping inspected Jilin Province on Wednesday. (Xinhua/Ju Peng)

　　2020 年 8 月 18 日至 21 日，中共中央总书记、国家主席、中央军委主席习近平在安徽省考察。图为 18 日下午，习近平在阜阳市阜南县红亮箱包有限公司察看车间生产线，了解企业灾后恢复生产和受灾群众、贫困群众就业情况。（新华社记者鞠鹏摄）

President Xi Jinping, also general secretary of the CPC Central Committee and chairman of the CMC, inspects the production line and learns about post-flood production recovery and the employment of local flood-affected and impoverished people at a luggage and bag manufacturer in Funan County, east China's Anhui Province, Aug. 18, 2020. Xi made an inspection tour in Anhui from Aug. 18 to 21, 2020. (Xinhua/Ju Peng)

2021 年 4 月 25 日至 27 日，中共中央总书记、国家主席、中央军委主席习近平在广西考察。图为 27 日上午，习近平在南宁市广西民族博物馆外，同参加三月三"歌圩节"民族文化活动的各族群众亲切交流。（新华社记者谢环驰摄）

President Xi Jinping, also general secretary of the CPC Central Committee and chairman of the CMC, talks to people of different ethnic groups who are participating in festive activities outside the Anthropology Museum of Guangxi in the city of Nanning, south China's Guangxi Zhuang Autonomous Region, April 27, 2021. Xi made an inspection trip to south China's Guangxi Zhuang Autonomous Region from April 25 to April 27. (Xinhua/Xie Huanchi)

2021年7月21日至23日，中共中央总书记、国家主席、中央军委主席习近平来到西藏，祝贺西藏和平解放70周年，看望慰问西藏各族干部群众。图为21日下午，习近平在林芝市巴宜区林芝镇嘎拉村，同村民达瓦坚参一家人围坐在客厅里聊家常。（新华社记者李学仁摄）

Chinese President Xi Jinping, also general secretary of the Communist Party of China (CPC) Central Committee and chairman of the Central Military Commission, chats with the Dawa Gyaltsen family in their living room at Galai Village of Nyingchi, southwest China's Tibet Autonomous Region, July 21, 2021. Xi visited the Tibet Autonomous Region from Wednesday to Friday. He extended congratulations to the 70th anniversary of Tibet's peaceful liberation and visited officials and ordinary people of various ethnic groups. (Xinhua/Li Xueren)

扶贫足迹

Poverty Alleviation Footprint

★ ★ ★ ★ ★

党的十八大以来，习近平总书记顶风雪、冒酷暑、踏泥泞，翻山越岭，跋山涉水，多次国内考察涉及扶贫，走遍全国 14 个集中连片特困地区，先后到 24 个贫困村调研。作为人民领袖，习近平总书记在扶贫工作上倾注了大量的情感和心力。

Since the 18th CPC National Congress, General Secretary Xi Jinping has braved the wind and snow, the heat and the cold, climbed mountains and waded through rivers to inspect the poverty alleviation work around the country for many times, during which he visited each and every one of the 14 contiguous poor areas and 24 poor villages. As the leader of the people, General Secretary Xi held deep emotion for and devoted enormous efforts to poverty alleviation.

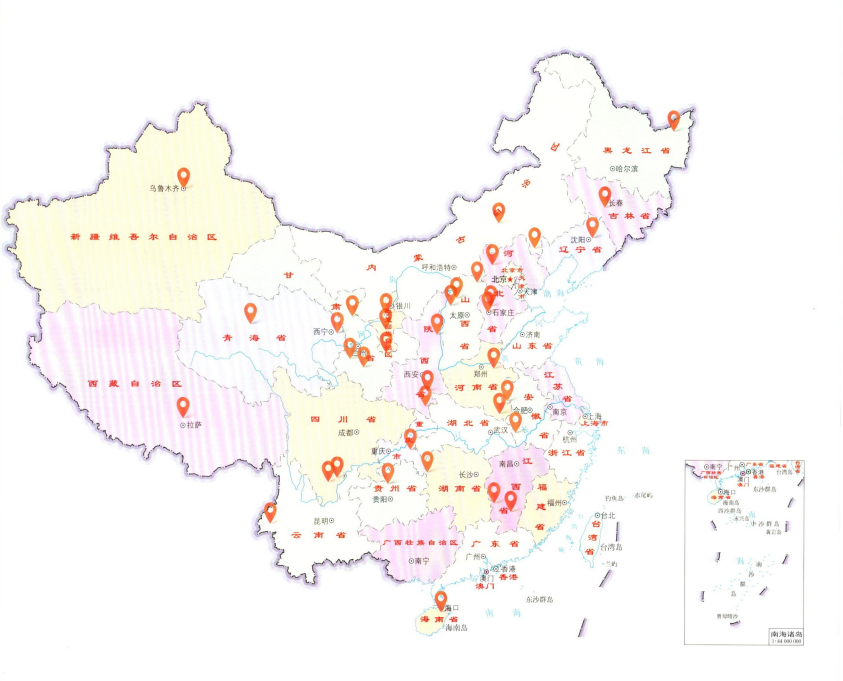

审图号：GS 京（2022）0928 号

日期	足迹	DATE	Footprint
2012 年 12 月 30 日	河北省阜平县顾家台村	Dec. 30, 2012.	Gujiatai Village of Longquanguan Township, Fuping County, north China's Hebei Province
2012 年 12 月 30 日	河北省保定市阜平县龙泉关镇骆驼湾村	Dec. 30, 2012.	Luotuowan Village of Longquanguan Township, Fuping County, north China's Hebei Province
2013 年 2 月 3 日	甘肃省临夏回族自治州东乡县高山乡布楞沟村	Feb. 3, 2013	Bulenggou Village of Dongxiang Autonomous County, northwest China's Gansu Province
2013 年 2 月 3 日	甘肃省定西市渭源县田家河乡元古堆村	Feb. 3, 2013	Yuangudui Village of Tianjiahe Township, Weiyuan County, northwest China's Gansu Province
2013 年 11 月 3 日	湖南省湘西州花垣县十八洞村	Nov. 3, 2013	Shibadong Village in Paibi Township of Huayuan County in the Tujia-Miao Autonomous Prefecture of Xiangxi, central China's Hunan Province
2013 年 11 月 3 日	湖南省湘西州凤凰县菖蒲塘村	Nov. 3, 2013	Changputang Village, Fenghuang County in central China's Hunan Province
2014 年 1 月 27 日	内蒙古锡林郭勒盟	Jan. 27, 2014	Xilingol League, north China's Inner Mongolia Autonomous Region
2014 年 3 月 17 日	河南省开封市兰考县东坝头乡张庄村	Mar. 17, 2014	Zhangzhuang Village, Lankao County in central China's Henan Province
2014 年 4 月 28 日	新疆果业集团有限公司	Apr. 28, 2014	a major fruit company in northwest China's Xinjiang Uygur Autonomous Region
2015 年 2 月 13 日	陕西省延安市延川县梁家河村	Feb. 13, 2015	Liangjiahe Village, Wen'anyi Township of Yanchuan County in northwest China's Shaanxi Province
2015 年 6 月 16 日	贵州省遵义市播州区花茂村	Jun. 16, 2015	Huamao Village of Fengxiang Township in Zunyi Count, southwest China's Guizhou Province

日期	足迹	DATE	Footprint
2016 年 2 月 2 日	江西井冈山市茅坪乡神山村	Feb. 2, 2016	Shenshan Village in Jinggangshan City, east China's Jiangxi Province
2016 年 4 月 24 日	安徽省金寨县花石乡大湾村	Apr. 24, 2016	Dawan Village of Huashi Township in Jinzhai County, east China's Anhui Province
2016 年 7 月 18 日	宁夏固原市泾源县大湾乡杨岭村	Jul. 18, 2016	Yangling Village,Jingyuan County in northwest China's Ningxia Hui Autonomous Region
2016 年 7 月 19 日	宁夏银川市永宁县闽宁镇原隆移民村	Jul. 19, 2016	Yuanlong Village of Minning Township in Yinchuan, capital of northwest China's Ningxia Hui Autonomous Region
2016 年 8 月 22 日	青海省海西蒙古族藏族自治州格尔木市唐古拉山镇长江源村	Aug. 22, 2016	Changjiangyuan Village, Golmud City in northwest China's Qinghai Province
2016 年 8 月 23 日	青海省海东市互助土族自治县五十镇班彦村	Aug. 23, 2016	Banyan Village of Wushi Township of Huzhu Tu Autonomous County, Qinghai Province
2017 年 1 月 24 日	河北张家口市张北县小二台镇德胜村	Jan. 24, 2017	Desheng Village, Xiaoertai Township of Zhangbei County, north China's Hebei Province
2017 年 6 月 21 日	山西省忻州市岢岚县赵家洼村	Jun. 21, 2017	Zhaojiawa Village of Kelan County in north China's Shanxi Province
2017 年 6 月 21 日	山西忻州市岢岚县宋家沟新村	Jun. 21, 2017	Songjiagou New Village, a resettlement site under a poverty alleviation program through relocation in Kelan County in north China's Shanxi Province
2018 年 2 月 11 日	四川凉山彝族自治州昭觉县解放乡火普村	Feb. 11, 2018	Huopu, a new village for relocated residents from poor areas, in Jiefang Township in Zhaojue County of Liangshan Yi Autonomous Prefecture

日期	足迹	DATE	Footprint
2018 年 2 月 11 日	四川省凉山州昭觉县三岔河乡三河村	Feb. 11, 2018	Sanhe Village of Sanchahe Township in Zhaojue County of Liangshan Yi Autonomous Prefecture, southwest China's Sichuan Province
2018 年 4 月 13 日	海南省海口市秀英区石山镇施茶村	Apr. 13, 2018	Shicha Village in Shishan Township of Xiuying District in Haikou City, south China's Hainan Province
2018 年 9 月 25 日	黑龙江省佳木斯市富锦市七星农场	Sept. 25, 2018	Qixing farm, northeast China's Heilongjiang Province
2018 年 9 月 28 日	辽宁省抚顺市东华园社区	Sept. 28, 2018	Donghuayuan, a resettlement community for residents from coal-mining area inFushun, northeast China's Liaoning Province
2019 年 4 月 15 日	重庆市石柱土家族自治县中益乡华溪村	Apr. 15, 2019	Huaxi Village of Shizhu Tujia Autonomous County, southwest China's Chongqing Municipality
2019 年 5 月 20 日	江西省赣州市于都县梓山镇潭头村	May. 20, 2019	Tantou Village in Yudu County, Ganzhou City, east China's Jiangxi Province
2019 年 7 月 15 日	内蒙古赤峰市喀喇沁旗河南街道马鞍山村	Jul. 15, 2019	Maanshan Village in Harqin Banner, Chifeng City, China's Inner Mongolia Autonomous Region
2019 年 8 月 21 日	甘肃省武威市古浪县黄花滩生态移民区富民新村	Aug. 21, 2019	Huanghuatan Community in Gulang County, northwest China's Gansu Province,
2019 年 9 月 17 日	河南省光山县文殊乡东岳村	Sept. 17, 2019	Dongyue Village. Guangshan County, China's Henan Province
2020 年 1 月 19 日	云南省腾冲市清水乡三家村中寨司莫拉佤族村	Jan. 19, 2020	a village of the Wa ethnic group in Qingshui Township in Tengchong City, southwest China's Yunnan Province

日期	足迹	DATE	Footprint
2020 年 4 月 20 日	陕西省商洛市柞水县小岭镇金米村	Apr. 20, 2020	Jinmi Village of Xiaoling Township in Zhashui County, Shangluo City, northwest China's Shaanxi Province
2020 年 4 月 21 日	陕西省安康市平利县老县镇	Apr. 21, 2020	Laoxian Township, Pingli County in Ankang City, northwest China's Shaanxi Province
2020 年 5 月 11 日	山西省大同市云州区	May. 11, 2020	Yunzhou District of Datong City, north China's Shanxi Province
2020 年 6 月 8 日	宁夏吴忠市红寺堡区红寺堡镇弘德村	Jun. 8, 2020	Hongde Village in Wuzhong City, northwest China's Ningxia Hui Autonomous Region
2020 年 7 月 23 日	吉林省长春市宽城区团山街道长山花园社区	Jul. 23, 2020	a residential community in Changchun, northeast China's Jilin Province
2020 年 8 月 18 日	安徽省阜南县红亮箱包有限公司	Aug. 18, 2020	a luggage and bag manufacturer in Funan County, east China's Anhui Province
2021 年 7 月 22 日	西藏拉萨市老城区的八廓街	Jul. 22, 2021	at Barkhor Street in Lhasa, southwest China's Tibet Autonomous Region

PART II

第二部分

脱贫·攻坚

POVERTY ALLEVIATION

脱贫攻坚战的冲锋号已经吹响。我们要立下愚公移山志，咬定目标、苦干实干，坚决打赢脱贫攻坚战，确保到 2020 年所有贫困地区和贫困人口一道迈入全面小康社会。

——2015 年 11 月 27 日至 28 日，习近平在中央扶贫开发工作会议上强调

脱贫攻坚是一场必须打赢打好的硬仗，是我们党向全国人民作出的庄严承诺。一诺千金。

——2018 年 2 月 12 日，习近平在打好精准脱贫攻坚战座谈会上的讲话

We have sounded a clarion call in the battle against poverty. To win this battle, we should have firm resolve and solid goals, and work hard with a down-to-earth spirit, to bring reasonable prosperity to all poverty-stricken areas and individuals by 2020.
—Xi Jinping makes the remarks at the Central Conference on Poverty Alleviation and Development on Nov. 27 and 28, 2015.

We must win the tough battle against poverty, as our Party has made a solemn promise to the people. We must be true to our promise.
—Xi Jinping said at a seminar on targeted poverty elimination on Feb. 12, 2018.

　　2015 年 6 月 16 日至 18 日，中共中央总书记、国家主席、中央军委主席习近平在贵州调研。图为 16 日下午，习近平在遵义县枫香镇花茂村的现代高效农业智能温控大棚，向正在劳动的村民了解增收致富情况。（新华社记者黄敬文摄）

Presient Xi Jinping, also general secretary of the CPC Central Committee and chairman of the CMC, visits a greenhouse using intelligent temperature control technology, at Huamao Village of Fengxiang Township in Zunyi County, southwest China's Guizhou Province, June 16, 2015, during an inspection tour in Guizhou from June 16 to 18, 2015. (Xinhua/Huang Jingwen)

2020 年 6 月 16 日无人机拍摄的贵州省遵义市播州区花茂村。（新华社记者陶亮摄）

The photo, taken with a drone on June 16, 2020, shows the Huamao Village in Bozhou District under Zunyi City of Guizhou Province. (Xinhua/Tao Liang)

　　2016 年 2 月 1 日至 3 日，中共中央总书记、国家主席、中央军委主席习近平来到江西，看望慰问广大干部群众和驻赣部队。图为 2 月 2 日，习近平在井冈山市茅坪乡神山村给乡亲们拜年，祝乡亲们生活幸福、猴年吉祥。（新华社记者谢环驰摄）

Presient Xi Jinping, also general secretary of the CPC Central Committee and chairman of the CMC, extends holiday greetings to villagers while visiting Shenshan Village in Jinggangshan City, east China's Jiangxi Province on Feb. 2, 2016. Xi extended holiday greetings to local residents and Jiangxi-based troops during his tour in Jiangxi from Feb. 1 to 3, 2016. (Xinhua/Xie Huanchi)

2020 年 1 月 15 日，在江西省井冈山市茅坪乡神山村，村民左秀发（右）向来村里旅游的游客介绍自家用毛竹制作的笔筒。（新华社记者彭昭之摄）

Zuo Xiufa (R) introduces to tourists his pen container made of bamboo at the village of Shenshan, Maoping Township, Jinggangshan City, east China's Jiangxi Province, Jan. 15, 2020. (Xinhua/Peng Zhaozhi)

2016 年 11 月 10 日拍摄的江西省井冈山市茅坪乡神山村全景。（新华社记者周密摄）

Aerial photo taken on Nov. 10, 2016 presents a panoramic view of Shenshan Village of Maoping Township in Jinggangshan, east China's Jiangxi Province. (Xinhua/Zhou Mi)

2017年1月24日，中共中央总书记、国家主席、中央军委主席习近平来到河北省张家口市，看望慰问基层干部群众，考察脱贫攻坚工作。图为习近平在张北县小二台镇德胜村徐海成家同村干部和村民代表座谈。（新华社记者兰红光摄）

Presient Xi Jinping, also general secretary of the CPC Central Committee and chairman of the CMC, talks with villagers and local cadre at the home of villager Xu Haicheng in Desheng Village, Xiaoertai Township of Zhangbei County, north China's Hebei Province, during his inspection tour on poverty alleviation work, Jan. 24, 2017. (Xinhua/Lan Hongguang)

2020 年 6 月 23 日无人机拍摄的河北省张北县德胜村村民在村里的光伏电站清理发电板。（新华社记者牟宇摄）

Aerial photo shows that villagers clean photovoltaic panels at a solar power station of Desheng Village in Zhangbei County of north China's Hebei Province, June 23, 2020. (Xinhua/Mou Yu)

　　2018 年 2 月 11 日，中共中央总书记、国家主席、中央军委主席习近平在凉山彝族自治州昭觉县解放乡易地扶贫搬迁新村火普村同乡亲们亲切握手。（新华社记者鞠鹏摄）

Chinese President Xi Jinping, also general secretary of the Communist Party of China Central Committee and chairman of the CMC, shakes hands with villagers as he visits Huopu, a new village for relocated residents from poor areas, in Jiefang Township in Zhaojue County of Liangshan Yi Autonomous Prefecture, southwest China's Sichuan Province, Feb. 11, 2018. (Xinhua/Ju Peng)

2018 年，四川省昭觉县解放乡火普村，群众全部住上新房。
（新华社记者蒋作平摄）

People move into new houses in Huopu Village of Jiefang Township in Zhaojue County, southwest China's Sichuan Province, in 2018. (Xinhua/Jiang Zuoping)

2019 年 3 月 13 日，"精准扶贫感恩连"在云南香格里拉市五境乡开展植树活动。（新华社记者胡超摄）
Tree planting activity was held on March 13, 2019 in Wujing Township of Shangri-La City in Yunnan Province amid efforts for targeted poverty alleviation. (Xinhua/Hu Chao)

　　2017 年 1 月 11 日，云南省墨江哈尼族自治县那哈乡的哈尼族扶贫工作队员周晓聪在查看乡里建档立卡贫困户的精准扶贫资料。（新华社记者胡超摄）

Zhou Xiaocong, a member of a poverty relief team, checks information about registered impoverished households in Mojiang Hani Autonomous County, southwest China's Yunnan Province, Jan. 11, 2017. (Xinhua/Hu Chao)

　　2018 年 5 月 3 日，青海省门源回族自治县大湾村村民李生祥在展示他的金融扶贫服务卡和贫困户信用证。（新华社发　王金金摄）

Li Shengxiang from Dawan Village of Menyuan Hui Autonomous County, northwest China's Qinghai Province, holds cards registering his information for preferential bank loans under the local poverty relief program, May 3, 2018. (Xinhua/Wang Jinjin)

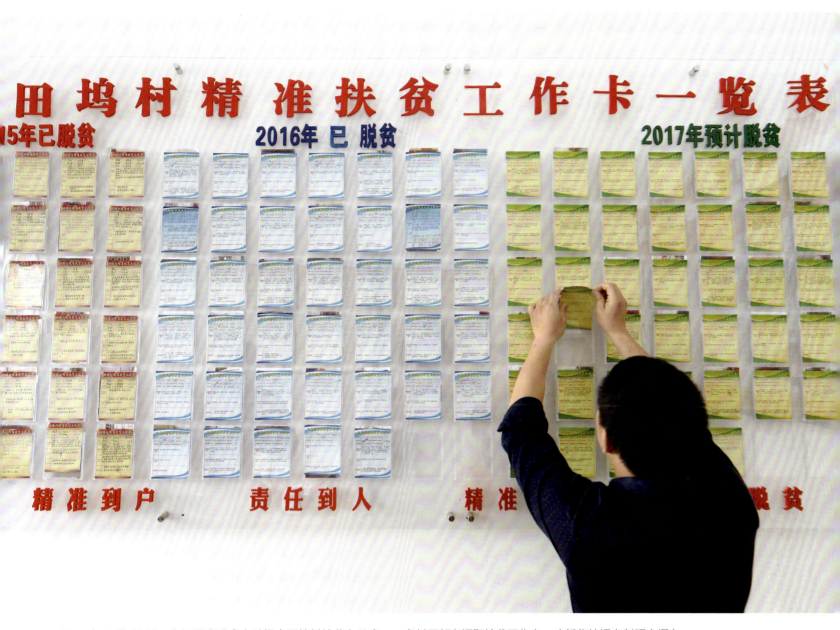

2017 年 4 月 10 日，在江西省瑞金市叶坪乡田坞村扶贫办公室，一名村干部在调取扶贫工作卡。（新华社记者彭昭之摄）

A village official picks up a card with information of a poor household in the poverty reduction office of Tianwu Village, Yeping Township, Ruijin City, east China's Jiangxi Province, on April 10, 2017. (Xinhua/Peng Zhaozhi)

　　吉日木图是内蒙古自治区苏尼特右旗赛罕乌力吉苏木脑干塔拉嘎查的牧民，多年来一直在外地打工。2014 年，他与乌仁塔娜结婚后回到家乡，所有资产只有 3800 亩草场和不到 50 只羊。小两口被苏木评定为建档立卡贫困户，旗里确定专门的干部帮他们脱贫。图为 2017 年 7 月 12 日，苏尼特右旗农牧业局副局长、嘎查第一书记乌日娜（左二）和吉日木图的脱贫包扶责任人、旗农技推广站站长武玉柱（右一）在了解吉日木图目前的生产情况。（新华社记者任军川摄）

Local officials chat with Jirumt (2nd R) and his wife Urantanaa (1st from the left), an impoverished couple from Sunite Right Banner, north China's Inner Mongolia Autonomous Region, to learn about their production situation, July 12, 2017. (Xinhua/Ren Junchuan)

　　云南省墨江哈尼族自治县是我国唯一的哈尼族自治县，当地山区半山区占 99.8%，是典型的集中连片特困地区，脱贫攻坚任务十分艰巨。2016 年年初全县有建档立卡贫困乡镇 7 个、贫困村 53 个、贫困人口 60749 人，贫困发生率达 20.06%。图为 2017 年 1 月 11 日，墨江哈尼族自治县那哈乡那苏村的哈尼族村民周军荣（右）和妻子张布背在查看扶贫手册。当地政府为建档立卡的贫困户都制作了扶贫手册。（新华社记者蔺以光摄）

Zhou Junrong, a villager from Mojiang Hani Autonomous County, southwest China's Yunnan Province, and his wife Zhang Bubei read a poverty alleviation handbook provided by the local government for registered impoverished households, Jan. 11, 2017. (Xinhua/Lin Yiguang)

2020 年 4 月 29 日，贵州省沿河土家族自治县思渠镇边疆村的扶贫干部晏飞（前）和钱鑫步行查看水源点。（新华社发　崔伟摄）

Local poverty relief officials Yan Fei (front) and Qian Xin, walk to check the water source in Yanhe Tujia Autonomous County, southwest China's Guizhou Province, April 29, 2020. (Xinhua/Cui Wei)

广西大化瑶族自治县板升乡八好村驻村第一书记韦德王和同事们一道带领群众争分夺秒决战贫困。图为 2019 年 12 月 16 日，韦德王（右一）和群众在搬运材料，准备修建水柜。（新华社记者黄孝邦摄）

Wei Dewang (1st R), first Party secretary of Bahao Village, prepares construction materials with villagers for a water storage project in the village of Dahua Yao Autonomous County, Guangxi Zhuang Autonomous Region, Dec. 16, 2019. Wei and his colleagues lead the villagers to race against the time to win the decisive battle of eliminating poverty. (Xinhua/Huang Xiaobang)

广西大化瑶族自治县是国家扶贫开发工作重点县，大部分贫困人口生活在石漠化大石山区，生存条件恶劣，生态环境脆弱，群众靠水柜攒雨水供人畜饮用。图为 2019 年 11 月 14 日无人机拍摄的江南乡上和村群众的家庭水柜。（新华社记者黄孝邦摄）

An aerial photo taken on Nov. 14, 2019 shows the water conservancy facilities at Shanghe Village, Dahua Yao Autonomous County in south China's Guangxi Zhuang Autonomous Region. Most impoverished people in the county live in mountainous areas suffering from rocky desertification, poor living conditions and weak ecological environment. Local people build water storage facilities to collect raindrops for drinking water. (Xinhua/Huang Xiaobang)

为彻底解决山区果农因旱少收无收而返贫的问题，广西百色市右江区投入 3000 多万元在山区芒果种植生产基地修建引调提水工程、芒果节水灌溉工程、抗旱备用井等多个"山顶引灌"工程。图为 2016 年 1 月 17 日航拍的永乐镇晚旧村芒果山上正在修建的引灌蓄水池。（新华社发　韦万忠摄）

An aerial photo taken on Jan. 17, 2016 shows a reservoir under construction in Wanjiu Village in Yongle Township in Baise City in south China's Guangxi Zhuang Autonomous Region. Local authorities have invested more than 30 million yuan (about 4.3 million U.S. dollars) building many "mountaintop irrigation" projects in the mango fields in the mountains to stop fruit farmers from falling back to poverty due to drought and lack of harvest. (Xinhua/Wei Wanzhong)

2019 年 6 月 30 日，在广西融水苗族自治县乌英苗寨，驻村第一书记韦桂华（右四）、党员梁成兵（右三）、梁志新（左二）带领村民维修河堤。（新华社记者黄孝邦摄）

Photo taken on June 30, 2019 shows Wei Guihua (4th R), secretary of the Communist Party of China local branch, carries a stone with Party members and villagers to reinforce a river dike in Wuying, an ethnic Miao village, Rongshui Miao Autonomous County, south China's Guangxi Zhuang Autonomous Region. (Xinhua/Huang Xiaobang)

　　近年来，"四好农村路"建设为农村带来了人气财气，凝聚了基层民心。以农村公路为依托，各地结合自身优势特点，探索出了"公路＋互联网""公路＋特色产业""公路＋乡村旅游"等发展模式，为乡村振兴提供了新助力。图为 2018 年 1 月 24 日用无人机航拍的四川省小金县老营乡尹家大坪葡萄基地。（新华社记者才扬摄）

A bird's-eye view of a vineyard in Laoying Township of Xiaojin County, southwest China's Sichuan Province, Jan. 24, 2018. Over the past few years, infrastructure improvement has injected new impetus into rural development. (Xinhua/Cai Yang)

2017 年 2 月 8 日，贵州省榕江县忠诚镇郊外的乡村公路。（新华社记者刘续摄）

A car drives on a country road outside Zhongcheng Township in Rongjiang County in southwest China's Guizhou Province, Feb. 8, 2017. (Xinhua/Liu Xu)

2020 年 3 月 15 日，搬家的车队在开道警车的引领下从云南省永善县大兴镇开往鲁甸县卯家湾易地扶贫安置区。（新华社记者江文耀摄）

Escorted by a police car, villagers are moving to their new homes at the Maojiawan resettlement site for impoverished people in Ludian County, southwest China's Yunnan Province, March 15, 2020. (Xinhua/Jiang Wenyao)

2018 年 9 月 29 日无人机拍摄的兰渝铁路甘肃陇南境内的汉王特大桥（右）与高速公路及国道交错。（新华社记者陈斌摄）

Aerial photo taken on Sept. 29, 2018 shows the Hanwang Bridge (R) on Lanzhou-Chongqing Railway in Longnan City, northwest China's Gansu Province. (Xinhua/Chen Bin)

2019 年 4 月 18 日无人机拍摄的安徽省霍山县太阳乡的大别山旅游扶贫快速通道。（新华社记者刘军喜摄）

Aerial photo taken on April 18, 2019 shows the special tourism poverty alleviation passageway of the Dabieshan Mountain in Taiyang Township of Huoshan County, east China's Anhui Province. (Xinhua/Liu Junxi)

　　2019 年 9 月 3 日无人机拍摄的广西融水苗族自治县乌英苗寨，群众在帮助贫困户梁秀金修建新木楼。（新华社记者黄孝邦摄）

People help impoverished villager Liang Xiujin build a wooden house at a village of Rongshui Miao Autonomous County, south China's Guangxi Zhuang Autonomous Region, Sept. 3, 2019. (Xinhua/Huang Xiaobang)

左图：2019 年 6 月 21 日，云南省贡山独龙族怒族自治县独龙江乡迪政当村独龙族的"文面女"李文仕（前排左）一家合影；右图：李文仕和其他村民的房子，这些房子是当地政府在 2011 年统一修建的。（新华社记者江文耀摄）

Combo photo taken on June 21, 2019 shows a family photo of Li Wenshi (L front), a woman of Dulong ethnic group, and houses built in 2011 by local government for Li and other villagers at Dizhengdang Village of Dulongjiang Township, Drung-Nu Autonomous County of Gongshan, southwest China's Yunnan Province. (Xinhua/Jiang Wenyao)

2019 年 8 月 28 日无人机拍摄的广西田东县思林镇易地扶贫搬迁安置点。（新华社记者曹祎铭摄）

Aerial photo shows that a poverty relief relocation site sits at Silin Township in Tiandong County, south China's Guangxi Zhuang Autonomous Region, Aug. 28, 2019. (Xinhua/Cao Yiming)

2020 年 3 月 15 日，云南省鲁甸县的卯家湾易地扶贫安置区。（新华社记者江文耀摄）

Aerial photo taken on March 15, 2020 shows the Maojiawan resettlement area for impoverished people in Ludian County, Yunnan Province. (Xinhua/Jiang Wenyao)

在 2018 年的易地扶贫搬迁中，家住贵州省安顺市西秀区岩腊乡龙潭村格沙苗寨的 6 岁女孩吉雪，与家人一起从缺水、耕地少、海拔高的格沙苗寨搬迁至 50 公里外的西秀区工业园区易地扶贫搬迁安置点——彩虹社区。社区内建有从幼儿园到初中的学校等便民配套设施。（新华社发　杨文斌摄）

Six-year-old Ji Xue and her ethnic Miao family move 50 km away from the inhospitable Gesha Village, where both water and arable land are scarce, to Rainbow Community that has kindergartens, schools and a full range of amenities in Xixiu Industrial Park of Anshun City, southwest China's Guizhou Province in 2018. (Xinhua/Yang Wenbin)

2018 年 2 月 12 日无人机航拍的贵州省龙里县易地扶贫搬迁县级集中安置点——冠山街道奋进社区。（新华社记者陶亮摄）

A bird's-eye view of Fenjin Residential Community in Guanshan Neighborhood, Longli County, southwest China's Guizhou Province, on Feb. 12, 2018. The community houses residents relocated from inhospitable poor areas. (Xinhua/Tao Liang)

　　自 2016 年以来，广西在总结乡村医生签约服务试点经验的基础上，全面推开乡村医生签约服务，提供健康教育处方和健康指导，健康扶贫取得阶段性成效。图为 2019 年 10 月 12 日，防城港市防城区扶隆镇那果村的乡村医生黄霖在为村民检查身体，整理健康档案。（新华社记者曹祎铭摄）

Rural doctor Huang Lin checks the physical condition of locals and files their health record at Naguo Village, Fangchenggang City in south China's Guangxi Zhuang Autonomous Region, Oct. 12, 2019. Based on experience gathered from pilot programs of contracted rural doctor services, Guangxi put in place the service across the region since 2016 providing grassroots health service. (Xinhua/Cao Yiming)

2017 年 10 月 20 日，在江西省永新县里田镇江南村，里田镇卫生院的医务人员在贫困户岩龙兰的家中展示家庭医生签约服务协议书。（新华社记者彭昭之摄）

A medical worker from a local health center displays an agreement of family doctor services on Oct. 20, 2017, at Yan Longlan's home at Jiangnan Village of Litian Township in Yongxin County, east China's Jiangxi Province. (Xinhua/Peng Zhaozhi)

2019 年 9 月 3 日，宁夏银川市永宁县闽宁镇原隆村卫生室，村民在看病。（新华社记者王鹏摄）

Villagers come to see the doctor in a clinic at Yuanlong Village of Minning Town in Yinchuan City, northwest China's Ningxia Hui Autonomous Region, Sept. 3, 2019. (Xinhua/Wang Peng)

河北阜平县是革命老区。近年来，阜平县积极推进健康扶贫模式，在基本医保、大病保险、医疗救助"三重保障线"基础上，财政投入资金，为困难群众提供防贫保险。同时，乡镇卫生院、村卫生室联合组队，定期上门问诊，保障困难群众享有基本医疗卫生服务。图为 2020 年 4 月 15 日，河北阜平县龙泉关镇顾家台村村医薄利走在出诊的路上。（新华社记者王晓摄）

Rural doctor Bo Li is on his way to a home visit to Gujiatai Village, Fuping County in north China's Hebei Province, April 15, 2020. In recent years, Fuping has been actively promoting the health poverty alleviation at grassroots level through basic medical insurance, serious disease insurance and medical assistance to provide poverty prevention insurance for poor people. (Xinhua/Wang Xiao)

　　为了扶贫先扶志，扶贫必扶智，广西成千上万的教师长年累月坚守在大山深处教书育人的讲台上。图为 2017 年 9 月 7 日，"挑书先生"韦志杰老师在大化瑶族自治县雅龙乡温和村通往巴丁教学点的路上挑书前行。（新华社记者周华摄）

Teacher Wei Zhijie shoulders books on his way to school at Wenhe Village, Dahua Yao Autonomous County in south China's Guangxi Zhuang Autonomous Region, Sept. 7, 2017. Thousands of teachers stick to their posts in the mountainous areas in Guangxi. (Xinhua/Zhou Hua)

国务院新闻办公室
THE STATE COUNCIL INFORMATION OFFICE, P.R.C.

近年来，全国已有近 11 万家民营企业精准帮扶 12.71 万个村，带动和惠及 1500 余万建档立卡贫困人口，参与规模之大、帮扶范围之广、投入力度之强前所未有。图为 2020 年 11 月 20 日，国务院新闻办公室在北京举行中外记者见面会，四位民营企业家代表围绕"万企帮万村——精准扶贫的民企行动"与中外记者见面交流。（新华社发　刘健摄）

Four private entrepreneurs exchange views with Chinese and foreign journalists about private enterprises'actions on targeted poverty alleviation, during a press conference hold by the State Council Information Office of China in Beijing, November 20, 2020. In recent years, nearly 110,000 private enterprises across the country have taken part in pairing assistance programs that have assisted 127,100 villages and benefited more than 15 million poor population. The scale of participation, the scope of assistance and the intensity of investment have been unprecedented. (Xinhua/Liu Jian)

图为 2018 年 9 月 3 日拍摄的云南省泸水市大兴地镇维拉坝珠海社区的格力小学。（新华社发）

In the picture, taken on September 3, 2018, is the Gree primary school. (Xinhua)

2019 年 9 月 4 日，湖南省花垣县十八洞小学一年级学生施蓉娅在上课时认真听讲。（新华社记者陈泽国摄）

Shi Rongya, a first-grade student, attends class in a primary school of Huayuan County, central China's Hunan Province, Sept. 4, 2019. (Xinhua/Chen Zeguo)

2013年9月10日，青海省治多县索加乡寄宿小学，学生们领到太阳能多功能便携灯后，在明亮的教室里上了第一堂课。（新华社记者何俊昌摄）

Students of a boarding primary school attend class with light for the first time after receiving solar-power portable lamps in Suojia Township in Zhiduo County, northwest China's Qinghai Province, Sept. 10, 2013. (Xinhua/He Junchang)

2019 年 10 月 9 日，宁夏泾源县泾河源镇白面民族小学师生在课堂教学的同时，与当地高峰村、白吉村教学点的学生进行网络在线互动。（新华社记者冯开华摄）

Students of a primary school in Jingheyuan Township communicate with students of other teaching outlets at local villages of Gaofeng and Baiji via webcam at class in Jingyuan County, northwest China's Ningxia Hui Autonomous Region, Oct. 9, 2019. (Xinhua/Feng Kaihua)

2020年4月30日，贵州省关岭县纸厂村村委会副主任张兴燚在刺梨基地查看刺梨长势。（新华社记者蒋成摄）

Zhang Xingyi, a village official, checks the growth of roxburgh rose fruits at a growing base in Zhichang Village, Guanling County, southwest China's Guizhou Province, April 30, 2020. (Xinhua/Jiang Cheng)

2019年10月28日，云南省怒江傈僳族自治州福贡县马吉乡木加甲村村民将采摘的草果装筐。（新华社发　杨雪辉摄）

Villagers collect the fruits they pick in Mujiajia Village, Maji Township, Fugong County, Nujiang Lisu Autonomous Prefecture, southwest China's Yunnan Province on Oct. 28, 2019. (Xinhua/Yang Xuehui)

金秋时节，甘肃省陇南市的 60 万亩油橄榄进入成熟采摘加工期。近年来，当地大力发展油橄榄产业，促进人们脱贫致富。图为 2018 年 10 月 30 日，在陇南市武都区汉王镇贾半山村，农户将采摘的油橄榄倒入收纳箱。（新华社记者范培珅摄）

Villagers collect the olives they pick at Jiabanshan Village, Hanwang Town, Longnan City, northwest China's Gansu Province on Oct. 30, 2018. The 40,000 hectares of olives in Longnan enter the harvest season in autumn. The olive industry has facilitated local poverty alleviation efforts. (Xinhua/ Fan Peishen)

2020 年 9 月，生活在来古冰川脚下的西藏昌都市八宿县然乌镇的村民开始秋收，金色的农田里，手扶拖拉机的马达声和村民的吆喝声交织成一段优美的劳动之歌。图为 9 月 10 日，西藏昌都市八宿县然乌镇康沙村的村民在收青稞。（新华社记者普布扎西摄）

Farmers harvest highland barley at Kangsar Village, Qamdo City of southwest China's Tibet Autonomous Region, Sept. 10, 2020. (Xinhua/Purbu Zhaxi)

近年来，四川省凉山彝族自治州布拖县依托当地苦荞加工企业建立接纳贫困户就业的"扶贫车间"，布拖县乌科乡、火烈乡 20 余个村还和当地企业以"企业＋基地＋农户"的模式发展苦荞种植与加工，带动当地 2000 余户农户（其中贫困户 583 户）增收。图为 2020 年 8 月 2 日，在布拖县火烈乡火烈村，当地群众在收割苦荞。（新华社记者江宏景摄）

Villagers harvest Tartary buckwheat at Huolie Village, Huolie Township, Butuo County in southwest China's Sichuan Province, Aug. 2, 2020. Tartary buckwheat industry in Butuo has helped over 2,000 rural households, including 583 impoverished households increase income in recent years. (Xinhua/ Jiang Hongjing)

2018 年 10 月 17 日，贵州省从江县高增乡占里村的村民在收割"香禾糯"稻谷。（新华社记者杨文斌摄）

Villagers harvest rice in Zhanli Village, Gaozeng Township, Congjiang County, southwest China's Guizhou Province, Oct. 17, 2018. (Xinhua/Yang Wenbin)

图为 2019 年 7 月 2 日拍摄的丹寨万达小镇。（新华社记者欧东衢摄）

Aerial photo taken on July 2, 2019 shows the view of Wanda town in Danzhai County, southwest China's Guizhou Province. (Xinhua/Ou Dongqu)

2020 年 6 月 6 日拍摄的贵州遵义市汇川区松林镇松林村山坡上的柑橘树、李子树等果树。（新华社记者刘智强摄）

Citrus and plum trees are planted on slopes of Songlin Village of Songlin Township, Zunyi City, southwest China's Guizhou Province, June 6, 2020. (Xinhua/Liu Zhiqiang)

2018 年 3 月 29 日拍摄的云南省威信县庙沟乡扎实沟村的猕猴桃种植基地一景。（新华社记者胡超摄）

A kiwifruit farm is seen in Zhashigou Village of Miaogou Township, Weixin County, in southwest China's Yunnan Province, March 29, 2018. (Xinhua/Hu Chao)

　　2016年10月14日，河北省新河县后沙洼村的菜农在现代农业产业园内运送刚刚采收的西红柿。该园区以蔬菜种植专业合作社为依托，采取合作社为主体，"致富带头人 + 贫困户"共同参股的新合作模式，帮助上万名贫困群众走上脱贫之路。（新华社记者牟宇摄）

Vegetable farmers deliver freshly harvested tomatoes in a modern agricultural industrial park in Houshawa Village, Xinhe County, in north China's Hebei Province, Oct. 14, 2016. The park adopts a new cooperation model with the specialized vegetable cooperatives helping tens of thousands of poor people shake off poverty. (Xinhua/Mou Yu)

　　2020 年 4 月 17 日，搬迁群众在云南省会泽县道成扶贫开发公司番茄种植大棚绕番茄秧。（新华社发　陈欣波摄）

Villagers tend tomato plants in Huize County in southwest China's Yunnan Province, April 17, 2020. (Xinhua/Chen Xinbo)

2017 年 5 月 18 日，重庆市黔江区濯水镇双龙村村民王孝顺（右）和陶素琼在桑园里查看桑叶。（新华社发　杨敏摄）

Villagers Wang Xiaoshun (R) and Tao Suqiong check mulberry leaves in a mulberry field in Shuanglong Village, Zhuoshui Township in Qianjiang District of southwest China's Chongqing Municipality, May 18, 2017. (Xinhua/Yang Min)

2017 年 6 月 26 日，收割机在陕西省富平县淡村镇杂交构树种植产业示范园内收割杂交构树。（新华社记者邵瑞摄）

A harvester reaps hybrid-paper mulberries at a farm in Dancun Town, Fuping County, northwest China's Shaanxi Province, June 26, 2017. (Xinhua/Shao Rui)

2020 年 3 月 4 日，河北省赞皇县土门乡龙堂院村的一位果农在大棚内管理樱桃。（新华社记者杨世尧摄）

A farmer tends cherry trees in Longtangyuan Village of Tumen Township, Zanhuang County, north China's Hebei Province, March 4, 2020. (Xinhua/Yang Shiyao)

河南省光山县把发展油茶作为实施精准扶贫的重要抓手，坚持走绿色发展道路，以"企业＋基地＋农户"的发展模式，把油茶产业作为富民的特色产业，推广新技术，发展深加工。图为 2020 年 8 月 25 日，村民在槐店乡一油茶园内除草。（新华社记者郝源摄）

Villagers weed in a camellia oil plantation in Huaidian Township of Guangshan County in central China's Henan Province, Aug. 25, 2020. Camellia oil plays an important role in targeted poverty alleviation in the county. (Xinhua/Hao Yuan)

安徽省六安市霍邱县城西湖乡积极调整农业产业结构，通过土地流转发展莲藕种植，并与相关企业合作建成规模化莲藕产业种植扶贫基地。图为 2020 年 8 月 26 日，采藕工人在西湖乡莲藕种植基地收获莲藕。（新华社记者韩晓雨摄）

Workers harvest lotus roots at a planting base in Xihu Township of Huoqiu County in east China's Anhui Province, Aug. 26, 2020. Xihu also works with enterprises to set up large-scale lotus root planting bases to help with poverty reduction. (Xinhua/Han Xiaoyu)

2018 年 4 月 27 日，贵州省毕节市大方县长石镇的村民在加工面条。（新华社发　罗大富摄）

A villager makes noodles in Changshi Township, Dafang County, southwest China's Guizhou Province, April 27, 2018. (Xinhua/Luo Dafu)

2018 年 10 月 31 日，甘肃省渭源县新寨镇新寨村，药农祁昌平在晾晒党参。（新华社记者陈斌摄）

Villager Qi Changping dries codonopsis pilosula, a plant used in traditional Chinese medicine, in Xinzhai Village of Xinzhai Township, Weiyuan County, northwest China's Gansu Province, Oct. 31, 2018. (Xinhua/Chen Bin)

2018 年 9 月 23 日，首个中国农民丰收节，拉萨市林周县松盘乡松盘村两名藏族农民在田间聊天。（新华社记者觉果摄）

Two Tibetan farmers chat with each other in the fields in Lhundrup County of Lhasa City, southwest China's Tibet Autonomous Region, on the first Chinese farmers' harvest festival, Sept. 23, 2018. (Xinhua/Jogod)

2019 年 10 月 15 日，广西隆安县一处安装有灯光补给系统的火龙果种植基地。（新华社记者曹祎铭摄）

A pitaya planting base is equipped with a light supply system in Long'an County, south China's Guangxi Zhuang Autonomous Region, Oct. 15, 2019. (Xinhua/Cao Yiming)

2020 年 3 月 14 日，陕西省宁强县巴山镇石坝子村脱贫户彭慧玲（右）在食用菌大棚里做直播。（新华社记者邵瑞摄）

Peng Huiling (R), a villager from Shibazi Village, Bashan Township, Ningqiang County in northwest China's Shaanxi Province, is seen in live streaming in a greenhouse planting edible mushrooms, March 14, 2020. (Xinhua/Shao Rui)

2019 年 10 月 25 日，在黑龙江省明水县一家食用菌企业，员工在采摘杏鲍菇。（新华社发　谢剑飞摄）

Staff workers of a local company pick mushrooms in Mingshui County, northeast China's Heilongjiang Province, Oct. 25, 2019. (Xinhua/Xie Jianfei)

2019 年 3 月 28 日，在黑龙江省宾县永和蔬菜生态现代产业园的阳光温室，工人在查看无土栽培的菜苗长势。（新华社记者王建威摄）

Workers check vegetable seedlings in a greenhouse at a modern industrial park in Binxian County in northeast China's Heilongjiang Province, March 28, 2019. (Xinhua/Wang Jianwei)

2019 年 10 月 22 日，陕西省延安市志丹县双河镇李家湾村村民在果园采摘苹果。（新华社记者陶明摄）

Villagers pick apples in an orchard at Lijiawan Village of Shuanghe Town, Zhidan County in northwest China's Shaanxi Province, Oct. 22, 2019. (Xinhua/Tao Ming)

2018 年 5 月 24 日无人机拍摄的陕西省延川县梁家河村山地苹果园。（新华社记者邵瑞摄）

The photo taken by a drone on May 24, 2018 shows an apple orchard in Liangjiahe Village of Yanchuan County in northwest China's Shaanxi Province. (Xinhua/Shao Rui)

2019 年 7 月 7 日拍摄的农民在贵州普安县地瓜镇屯上村的"扶贫茶园"里给茶苗施肥。（新华社记者杨文斌摄）

Farmers fertilize tea seedlings in a tea garden in Tunshang Village, Digua Township, Pu'an County in southwest China's Guizhou Province, July 7, 2019. (Xinhua/Yang Wenbin)

2016 年 10 月 12 日，河南省光山县槐店乡晏岗村农户在采摘油茶籽。（新华社记者李安摄）

Farmers pick camellia seeds in Yangang Village, Huaidian Township, Guangshan County in central China's Henan Province, Oct. 12, 2016. (Xinhua/Li An)

2020 年 4 月 24 日，茶农在陕西省平利县凤凰茶山采茶。（新华社发　李世锋摄）

Tea farmers pick tea leaves in the Fenghuang tea mountain in Pingli County in north China's Shaanxi Province, April 24, 2020. (Xinhua/Li Shifeng)

　　近年来，内蒙古各地举办多种以"马"为主题的体育、文化、旅游活动，吸引外来游客来体验蒙古族马文化，探索将蒙古马的保护和发展与促进牧民增收相结合。图为 2015 年 7 月 21 日，牧民在锡林浩特市宝力根苏木的草原上套马。（新华社记者任军川摄）

Herdsmen try to rope horses on the prairie at Xilinhot, north China's Inner Mongolia Autonomous Region, July 21, 2015. Various types of horse-themed sports, culture and tourism activities have been held across Inner Mongolia in recent years as part of the region's efforts to conserve and develop the Mongolian horses while increase the income of herdsmen, attracting tourists to the region to experience the horse culture of the Mongolian ethnicity. (Xinhua/Ren Junchuan)

2017 年 3 月 8 日，陕西省长武县亭口镇二厂村养驴场内，工作人员在给驴喂食。（新华社记者邵瑞摄）

A staff member feeds donkeys in a donkey farm in Erchang Village of Tingkou Township, Changwu County, northwest China's Shaanxi Province, March 8, 2017. (Xinhua/Shao Rui)

2017 年 10 月 29 日，在广西融水苗族自治县四荣乡江潭村，67 岁的贫困户戴邦林在养鸭场里。（新华社记者黄孝邦摄）

Sixty-seven-year-old Dai Banglin works at a duck farm in Jiangtan Village of Sirong Township in Rongshui Miao Autonomous County, south China's Guangxi Zhuang Autonomous Region, Oct. 29, 2017. (Xinhua/Huang Xiaobang)

2019 年 8 月 18 日，在广西融安县大良镇古兰村古兰屯养牛基地，68 岁的韦肇翠在观察自家养的牛。（新华社记者黄孝邦摄）

Sixty-eight-year-old Wei Zhaocui checks the cattle he raises in a cattle farm in Gulan Village of Daliang Township, Rong'an County, south China's Guangxi Zhuang Autonomous Region, Aug. 18, 2019. (Xinhua/Huang Xiaobang)

2020 年 3 月 11 日，无人机拍摄的工人在贵州省锦屏县铜鼓镇马台生态种鹅养殖基地投放草料。（新华社记者杨文斌摄）

A drone captures the moment that a farmer feeds geese at a breeding base in Tonggu Township of Jinping County, southwest China's Guizhou Province, March 11, 2020. (Xinhua/Yang Wenbin)

西藏类乌齐县平均海拔 4500 米左右，当地群众以放牧为生。这里草场丰美，牦牛肉品质高，但牧民单打独斗的经营方式在市场上不占优势。近年来，当地以"公司＋基地＋合作社＋农牧户"的模式，实施科学化养殖、精细化加工、产业化经营，牦牛产业实现转型升级，带动越来越多的群众增收致富。图为 2020 年 9 月 21 日，西藏昌都市类乌齐县滨达乡央宗村牦牛短期育肥示范基地的牦牛。（新华社记者詹彦摄）

Yaks stand at a farmhouse at a village in Riwoqe County, Qamdo City of southwest China's Tibet Autonomous Region on Sept. 21, 2020. Local people mainly live on grazing at Riwoqe County thanks to its abundant grassland with an average altitude of 4,500 meters above sea level. In recent years, local yak industry has been transformed and upgraded, thus helping more and more people raise income and become better off. (Xinhua/Zhan Yan)

2015 年 12 月 20 日，广西田东县隆祥兔业农民专业合作社工作人员在展示养殖的兔子。（新华社记者张爱林摄）

A staff member displays a rabbit raised in a specialized farmers' cooperative in Tiandong County, south China's Guangxi Zhuang Autonomous Region, Dec. 20, 2015. (Xinhua/Zhang Ailin)

甘肃省东乡族自治县在部分乡镇试点新的"羊产业"发展模式，通过政府补助和贴息贷款帮助养羊农户完成暖棚改造和扩大养殖规模，使养殖户从传统的家庭散养模式向现代规模经营转型。图为 2015 年 3 月 16 日，龙泉乡北庄岭村村民赵麦得在自家的暖棚里赶羊。（新华社记者陈斌摄）

Zhao Maide herds sheep in the brooder in Beizhuangling Village, Longquan Township, Dongxiang Autonomous County in northwest China's Gansu Province, March 16, 2015. The county pilots in some of its townships a development model driven by the sheep raising industry. With the help of government subsidies or subsidized loans, sheep raisers are able to renovate their sheep brooders and raise more sheep. (Xinhua/Chen Bin)

2020 年 3 月 10 日，工人在贵州省天柱县凤城街道石坪童子鸡养殖示范基地清理鸡舍。（新华社记者杨文斌摄）

A farmer cleans the chicken house of a breeding base at Fengcheng Community of Tianzhu County, southwest China's Guizhou Province, March 10, 2020. (Xinhua/Yang Wenbin)

甘肃省玛曲县持续推进甘南黄河重要水源补给生态功能区生态保护与建设，使玛曲湿地生态功能得到逐步恢复，成为甘南发展全域旅游的重要目的地。图为 2018 年 7 月 31 日，游客在湿地的观景步道上游览。（新华社记者陈斌摄）

Tourists walk on a boardwalk at a wetland in Maqu County of Gannan Tibetan Autonomous Prefecture, northwest China's Gansu Province, July 31, 2018. Wetlands in Maqu have seen gradual recovery in ecological functions and became important tourist attractions in Gannan. (Xinhua/Chen Bin)

通过大力改善乡村学校办学条件、实施建档立卡贫困户家庭学生 15 年免费教育、完善大学贫困生资助政策等多项举措，广西帮助贫困家庭拔掉穷根。图为 2017 年 9 月 4 日，大化瑶族自治县板升乡弄勇小学改造后的校园环境。（新华社记者黄孝邦摄）

An aerial view of Nongyong Primary School in Bansheng Township of Dahua Yao Autonomous County, south China's Guangxi Zhuang Autonomous Region, after its renovation, Sept. 4, 2017. Guangxi helped impoverished households root out poverty with a slew of measures including improving teaching conditions at rural schools, offering 15-year free education to students from poverty-stricken families, and providing financial support to college students from such families. (Xinhua/Huang Xiaobang)

2019 年 6 月 21 日拍摄的河北新河县新河镇六户村一角。（新华社记者王晓摄）

A view of Liuhu Village in Xinhe Township, Xinhe County of north China's Hebei Province, June 21, 2019. (Xinhua/Wang Xiao)

2017 年 8 月 12 日，在山西汾阳吕梁山高级护工培训基地护工实操间，张贵枝（右三）和学员们一起学习病患陪护知识。（新华社记者詹彦摄）

Zhang Guizhi (3rd R) and other care workers practice at a care worker training center in Fenyang City, north China's Shanxi Province, Aug. 12, 2017. (Xinhua/Zhan Yan)

贵州省纵深推进农村产业革命，并在医疗健康扶贫等方面持续发力，助力全省乡村脱贫振兴。图为 2019 年 2 月 28 日，医务人员在六盘水六枝特区郎岱镇卫生院给小朋友输液。（新华社记者陶亮摄）

A doctor puts a child on intravenous drip at a medical center in Langdai Township, Liupanshui City in southwest China's Guizhou Province, Feb. 28, 2019. Guizhou has been working to lift people out of poverty and vitalize rural areas by advancing industrial revolution and improving medical services across the countryside. (Xinhua/Tao Liang)

　　岳西县是大别山区国家扶贫开发工作重点县。近年来，岳西县立足当地特色，探索出产业扶贫、易地搬迁、兜底保障等"三主措施"，实现每村有一个以上致富主导产业，每户有一个以上脱贫产业项目。图为 2016 年 12 月 4 日，安徽省岳西县中关镇请寨村 41 户贫困户合建的光伏扶贫电站试运行发电。光伏扶贫是该县"十大产业"之一，让没有劳动能力的贫困户，每户每年稳定增收 3000 元。（新华社发　储青摄）

A photovoltaic power station, jointly built by 41 impoverished households, begins trial operation at Qingzhai Village of Yuexi County in east China's Anhui Province on Dec. 4, 2016. Photovoltaic poverty alleviation is one of the "ten major industries" in Yuexi to help poor households without working ability to increase their income by 3,000 yuan per year.(Xinhua/Chu Qing)

　　河北省北部地区的张家口和承德两市借助太阳能资源大力推进乡村光伏发电站精准扶贫项目。截至 2018 年年底，两市 10 个县共建成村级光伏扶贫电站 878 个，装机总容量 40.65 万千瓦，惠及 1180 个贫困村的 6 万多个贫困家庭。图为 2019 年 1 月 19 日，工人在张家口市怀安县头百户镇一光伏扶贫电站维护并网设备。（新华社记者杨世尧摄）

Workers maintain the in-grid equipment at a poverty-relief photovoltaic power station in Zhangjiakou City, north China's Hebei Province on Jan. 19, 2019. Zhangjiakou and Chengde, two cities in northern Hebei, are vigorously promoting targeted poverty alleviation projects of rural photovoltaic power stations. By the end of 2018, a total of 878 such power stations were established in the two cities, with a total installed capacity of 406,500 kilowatts, benefiting more than 60,000 impoverished families in 1,180 villages. (Xinhua/Yang Shirao)

2019 年 9 月拍摄的宁夏永宁县原隆村的光伏大棚。（新华社记者王鹏摄）

Photovoltaic greenhouses sit at Yuanlong Village, Yongning County, in northwest China's Ningxia Hui Autonomous Region, September 2019. (Xinhua/Wang Peng)

　　2014 年以来，河南省兰考县创新金融扶贫方式，推动政、银、企"三位一体"，贷款给企业发展扶贫产业，带动贫困户脱贫。截至 2015 年 11 月，精准扶贫人数超过 1000 人。图为工人袁排朵、王翠云夫妇在兰考县大河乐器有限公司车间里工作。（新华社记者冯大鹏摄）

Yuan Paiduo and Wang Cuiyun, a couple from Lankao County in central China's Henan Province, make musical instruments at a workshop. Since 2014, local government in Lankao has been teaming up with banks to help poverty-stricken households get rid of poverty by providing targeted financial support to businesses. As of November 2015, more than 1,000 people had benefited from the program. (Xinhua/Feng Dapeng)

　　在2015年11月召开的中央扶贫开发工作会议上，习近平总书记要求实施"五个一批"工程，第一个就是"发展生产脱贫一批"，立足当地资源，实现就地脱贫。而此前，他将"项目安排精准"列为扶贫"六个精准"之一。核桃扶贫，正是我国产业扶贫的缩影。图为2015年9月23日，云南省大姚县一家核桃产品加工厂内，工人在分拣核桃。（新华社记者王全超摄）

Workers sort walnuts at a processing plant in Dayao County, southwest China's Yunnan Province on Sept. 23, 2015. Poverty alleviation through planting walnuts is one of the measures picked by local authorities amid China's poverty alleviation efforts. (Xinhua/Wang Quanchao)

　　截至 2017 年年末，青海各项金融精准扶贫贷款余额 1125.96 亿元，同比增长 21.38%，其中个人精准扶贫贷款余额 35.88 亿元，同比增长 64.74%，"三有一无"贫困户获贷率达 54%。图为 2018 年 5 月 3 日门源农商银行工作人员（左）与当地村民交流，了解饲草合作社金融服务需求。（新华社发　王金金摄）

A local bank employee talks with local villagers to learn about the financial service needs of forage cooperatives in Menyuan Hui Autonomous County in northwest China's Qinghai Province, May 3, 2018. By the end of 2017, financial institutions in Qinghai granted 112.6 billion yuan, in poverty alleviation loans. (Xinhua/Wang Jinjin)

　　2018 年 5 月 3 日，青海省海北藏族自治州门源回族自治县西沙河村村民前往该村的惠农金融服务点办理业务。（新华社记者徐文婷摄）

A villager arrives at a financial service outlet at Xishahe Village, Haibei Tibetan Autonomous Prefecture in northwest China's Qinghai Province, May 3, 2018. (Xinhua/Xu Wenting)

　　为了让村民还贷、取款不用跑到乡上、县城，党的十九大代表、宁夏回族自治区吴忠市盐池县王乐井乡曾记畔村党支部书记朱玉国多方争取，宁夏黄河农村商业银行、邮政储蓄银行陆续在村部设立了综合服务点。图为 2017 年 9 月 20 日，在宁夏盐池县曾记畔村黄河农村商业银行综合网点，朱玉国（右）在为村民办理相关业务。（新华社记者李然摄）

Zhu Yuguo (R), Party chief of Zengjipan Village in northwest China's Ningxia Hui Autonomous Region, handles a villager's bank application at an outlet of the Yellow River Rural Commercial Bank, Sept. 20, 2017. Zhu, also a delegate to the 19th National Congress of the Communist Party of China, has been asking for the benefits of rural residents at Zengjipan Village, who used to trek to banks in township or county centers to pay loans or withdraw deposits. Thanks to his strenuous efforts, the Yellow River Rural Commercial Bank and the Postal Saving Bank of China have set up outlets at Zengjipan Village. (Xinhua/Li Ran)

　　广西融水苗族自治县将刺绣这一"指尖艺术"作为妇女实现脱贫致富的重要产业，积极发展"巾帼巧手经济"，加强对易地扶贫搬迁群众的就业技能培训，实现"搬出来、留得住、发展好"。图为 2019 年 11 月 18 日拍摄的妇女们在易地扶贫安置点苗家小镇"妇女之家巾帼扶贫车间"学习刺绣。（新华社记者黄孝邦摄）

Local women learn embroidery at a workshop at a relocation community for poverty alleviation in Rongshui Miao Autonomous County in South China's Guangxi Zhuang Autonomous Region, Nov. 18, 2019. The county actively develops handicraft economy and strengthens employment skills training for people who have been relocated from inhospitable areas to help them live a better life at their new home. (Xinhua/Huang Xiaobang)

　　2019 年 11 月 2 日宁夏同心县扶贫生产车间内，质量检测员在查看防护服样品。（新华社发　杨植森摄）

A quality inspector checks samples of protective clothing at a poverty alleviation workshop in Tongxin County in northwest China's Ningxia Hui Autonomous Region, Nov. 2, 2019. (Xinhua/Yang Zhisen)

近年来，贵州省雷山县大力创设非遗扶贫就业工坊，培育传承人，开发文创旅游产品，创造就业岗位，带动当地群众脱贫致富。图为 2020 年 4 月 10 日，雷山县宏鑫工艺品加工厂生产的藤编产品。（新华社记者郑明鸿摄）

Hongxin Craftwork Plant in Leishan County, southwest China's Guizhou Province, showcases its rattan products, April 10, 2020. Over the past years, Leishan has provided strong support to workshops leveraging intangible cultural heritage as a way to eradicate poverty. The practice has nurtured inheritors for the intangible cultural heritage, developed culture-inspired souvenirs and products, and helped create jobs and lift local people out of poverty. (Xinhua/Zheng Minghong)

2020 年 3 月 13 日，贵州省雷山县郎德镇也利村的村民在采摘吊脚楼里种植的香菇。（新华社记者杨文斌摄）

A villager from Yeli Village in Langde Town, Leishan County in southwest China's Guizhou Province, picks mushrooms in a stilted building, a distinctive architecture style of local Miao ethnic group, March 13, 2020. (Xinhua/Yang Wenbin)

2018 年 9 月 7 日，村民在广西宁明县浦瓜村扶贫车间组装电子产品。（新华社记者周华摄）

Villagers assemble electronic products at a poverty-relief workshop at Pugua Village, Ningming County in south China's Guangxi Zhuang Autonomous Region, Sept. 7, 2018.(Xinhua/Zhou Hua)

2017 年 12 月 28 日，在福建省古田县大桥镇的一家银耳生产企业，镇纪委书记雷冬铃（左二）向贫困户肖高需（右二）了解生产情况和家庭状况。（新华社记者魏培全摄）

Local official Lei Dongling (2nd L) asks Xiao Gaoxu (2nd R), who is from a poor household, about his production and family situation at a local tremella production enterprise at Daqiao Township of Gutian County in east China's Fujian Province, Dec. 28, 2017. (Xinhua/Wei Peiquan)

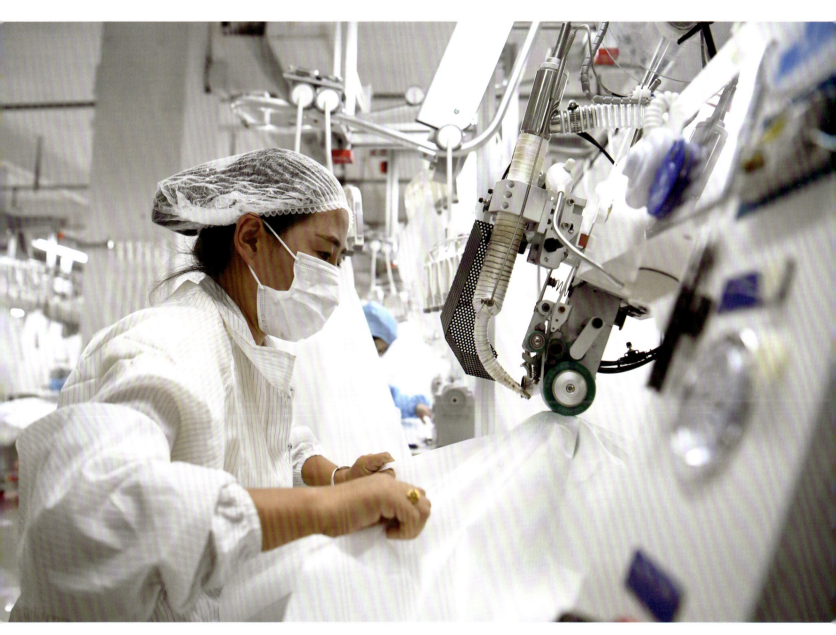

2020 年 8 月 9 日，甘肃拓奇扶贫车间的员工在服装加工生产线上作业。（新华社记者陈斌摄）

An employee works on a garment production line in a poverty alleviation workshop in northwest China's Gansu Province, Aug. 9, 2020. (Xinhua/Chen Bin)

2020 年 6 月 17 日，在四川省松潘县的"中国特产·阿坝州扶贫馆"里，两名从成都来到这里的 MCN 服务商团队成员通过京东直播平台，帮助松潘当地企业直播销售沙棘饮料等特产。（新华社记者沈伯韩摄）

Two e-commerce staff from Chengdu help a local enterprise in Songpan County in southwest China's Sichuan Province sell sea buckthorn beverages and other specialties through a livestreaming platform, June 17, 2020. (Xinhua/Shen Bohan)

2020 年 4 月 22 日，在陕西省平利县老县镇锦屏社区的社区工厂，一家企业负责人顾芝红（左一）向客人介绍产品。（新华社记者邵瑞摄）

Gu Zhihong (1st L), manager of an enterprise, introduces products to customers at a community factory in Laoxian Township, Pingli County in north China's Shaanxi Province, April 22, 2020. (Xinhua/Shao Rui)

2020 年 10 月 31 日，消费者在中国西部消费扶贫中心四川馆选购扶贫产品。当日，位于重庆市江北区北滨一路渔人湾码头的中国西部消费扶贫中心正式开馆。该中心占地面积约 1.5 万平方米，内设中国西部 11 个省（自治区）级馆、重庆市 33 个区县馆，以及扶贫产品展销中心、消费扶贫活动中心、集采配送中心、直播中心等。（新华社记者王全超摄）

Consumers purchase goods at the Sichuan Pavilion of the China Western Consumption Poverty Alleviation Center on Oct. 31, 2020. The center, located at the Fisherman's Bay Wharf, Chongqing, southwest China, opened on the same day. Covering an area of 15,000 square meters, it consists of 11 pavilions for China's western provinces and autonomous regions and 33 pavilions for Chongqing's districts and counties. (Xinhua/Wang Quanchao)

2020 年 10 月 31 日，中国西部消费扶贫中心西藏馆工作人员（左）向消费者介绍扶贫产品。（新华社记者王全超摄）

A worker (L) at the Tibet Pavilion of the China Western Consumption Poverty Alleviation Center promotes products from poor regions to consumers on Oct. 31, 2020. (Xinhua/Wang Quanchao)

　　江西上犹县寺下镇富足村有个远近闻名的"富足之家"，是一个集农副产品收购、销售为一体的消费扶贫平台，通过线下订购、线上直播的销售模式，拓宽农副产品销售渠道，增加农民收入。自 2018 年 6 月底运营以来，"富足之家"共帮助农户销售产品 46.8 万元。图为 2020 年 10 月 18 日，"富足之家"工作人员舒小小通过线上直播在销售农副产品。（新华社记者李鑫摄）

Photo shows Shu Xiaoxiao, a staff member of "Home of Abundance", sells agricultural and sideline products through livestreaming on Oct. 18, 2020. There is a well-known "Home of Abundance" in Fuzu Village, Shangyou County, Jiangxi Province. It is a poverty alleviation platform integrating the purchase and sales of agricultural and sideline products. It expands sales channels of agricultural and sideline products through offline ordering and online livestreaming sales, increasing farmers' income. Since June 2018 when it started operation, "Home of Abundance" has helped farmers sell products for 468,000 yuan. (Xinhua/Li Xin)

　　2020 年 7 月 30 日，在保定扶贫产品直供北京采购基地现场的展销会上，采购者在咨询扶贫农产品情况。（新华社记者陈钟昊摄）

At a trade fair of poverty alleviation products from Baoding city of north China's Hebei Province, consumers consult on agricultural products on July 30, 2020. (Xinhua/Chen Zhonghao)

2020 年 5 月 27 日，新疆和田玉石交易中心户外直播基地落成仪式在新疆和田玉石中心玉石产业园玉石交易市场举行。玉石交易中心户外直播基地将依托互联网优势推广和田的核桃、大枣、玫瑰花等名优特产，是助力打赢脱贫攻坚战的有力举措。图为 2020 年 5 月 27 日，两名女孩在扶贫助农直播活动中展示和田土特产。（新华社记者沙达提摄）

Photo shows two girls demonstrate the local specialties of Hotan in a live streaming themed poverty alleviation and farmer assistance on May 27, 2020. The inauguration ceremony of the outdoor streaming base of Xinjiang Hotan Jade Trading Center was held to promote Hotan's famous and special products such as walnuts, jujubes, and roses, which will effectively help win the battle against poverty. (Xinhua/Sadat)

近年来，在东西部扶贫协作机制下，福建省厦门市帮助甘肃省临夏回族自治州引进服装鞋帽、户外用品、文化旅游、农产品深加工等企业。目前，厦门市共帮助临夏州引进企业 57 家，援建扶贫车间 232 家，吸纳当地农民就地就近就业。图为 2020 年 10 月 31 日，在甘肃省临夏回族自治州永靖县刘家峡镇的一个扶贫车间里，工人在针织生产线上作业。（新华社发 史有东摄）

Photo shows workers on a knitting production line in a poverty alleviation workshop in Liujiaxia Town, Linxia Hui Autonomous Prefecture, Gansu Province on Oct. 31, 2020. In recent years, under the cooperation mechanism of poverty alleviation between the east and the west, Xiamen City in east China's Fujian Province has helped Linxia to attract companies in garment, footwear, outdoor products, cultural tourism, and deep processing of agricultural products. (Xinhua/Shi Youdong)

2019年5月22日，在位于湖北郧西县观音村的米高龙制鞋扶贫车间，村民在加工产品。在车间工作的村民平均每人每月可收入2500元左右。（新华社记者肖艺九摄）

Villagers earn about 2,500 yuan (about 363 U.S. dollars) a month at a shoe making workshop for poverty relief at Guanyin Village in Yunxi County, central China's Hubei Province, May 22, 2019. (Xinhua/Xiao Yijiu)

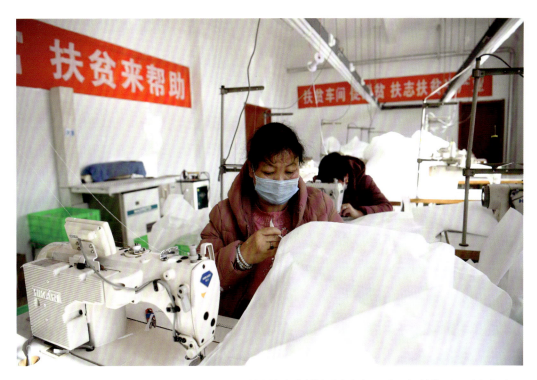

2020 年 3 月 11 日，村民在宁夏贺兰县洪广镇广荣村扶贫车间加工家居摆件外罩。（新华社记者王鹏摄）

Villagers process outer covers of home furnishing ornaments at a poverty alleviation workshop at Guangrong Village of Hongguang Township, Helan County in northwest China's Ningxia Hui Autonomous Region, March 11, 2020. (Xinhua/Wang Peng)

2020 年 6 月 2 日，密珍花在云南省泸水市大兴地镇维拉坝珠海社区数据线加工扶贫车间工作。（新华社发）

A villager works at a data cable processing workshop for poverty alleviation in Daxingdi Township of Lushui City in southwest China's Yunnan Province, June 2, 2020. (Xinhua)

2019 年 9 月 4 日，青海省互助土族自治县班彦新村村民在盘绣园内制作盘绣。（新华社记者张宏祥摄）

Villagers make special embroidery of Tu ethnic group at Banyan New Village, Huzhu Tu Autonomous County in northwest China's Qinghai Province, Sept. 4, 2019. (Xinhua/Zhang Hongxiang)

四川省泸州市叙永县采取"公司＋专业合作社＋农户＋基地"的模式，因地制宜发展大米产业，实施产业化扶贫项目，助力村民增收致富。图为 2020 年 8 月 26 日，黄坭镇黄坭村村民在抢收水稻。（新华社发　李欣摄）

Photo shows villagers in Huangni Village, Xuyong County, southwest China's Sichuan Province, harvest rice on Aug. 26, 2020. The local authorities adopt a model that integrates efforts by companies, professional cooperatives, farmers and production bases to develop the rice industry in accordance with local conditions. (Xinhua/Li Xin)

2020 年 4 月 8 日，在重庆市石柱县中益乡坪坝村，一名村民检查炕黄连之后的黄连干湿情况。（新华社记者刘潺摄）

A villager checks the condition of coptis, a traditional Chinese medical herb, at Pingba Village, Zhongyi Township of Shizhu Tujia Autonomous County, southwest China's Chongqing, April 8, 2020. (Xinhua/Liu Chan)

2020 年 5 月 14 日，在山西省大同市云州区西坪镇拍摄的晾晒好的黄花。（新华社发 柴婷摄）

Dried day lilies are stored in a house in Xiping Township, Datong City in north China's Shanxi Province, May 14, 2020. (Xinhua/Chai Ting)

2020 年 3 月 24 日，湖北省总工会在安陆市开展送外出务工者返岗专场活动。来自安陆市各地的数百名外出务工人员乘坐包车，直达广东深圳、东莞等地，有序返岗。（新华社记者胡虎虎摄）

Photo shows the Federation of Trade Unions of central China's Hubei Province launched a special event in Anlu City for outgoing migrant workers on March 24, 2020. Hundreds of migrant workers from Anlu took chartered buses bound for Shenzhen, Dongguan and other places in south China's Guangdong Province, returning to work in an orderly manner. (Xinhua/Hu Huhu)

　　成昆铁路线上的慢火车，往返于普雄和攀枝花之间，沿途停靠 26 个站，走满全程需要 9 个多小时，极大地解决了沿途群众的出行问题。大凉山的外出务工人员都是乘着这趟车踏出离家的第一步。图为 2020 年 10 月 4 日，在成昆铁路联合乡站下车的彝族群众。（新华社发　胡仲平摄）

Photo shows people from the Yi ethnic group getting off a train at Lianhe Township Station of the Chengdu-Kunming Railway on Oct. 4, 2020. The slow train service between Puxiong and Panzhihua has 26 stations along the Chengdu-Kunming Railway, with a full journey taking more than 9 hours. It meets travel demands of people along the way. Outgoing migrant workers in Daliang Mountain take this train in their first step to the outside. (Xinhua/Hu Zhongping)

2020 年 5 月 14 日，湖北、山东通过网络视频实时连线，完成《鄂鲁支持贫困劳动力外出务工暨劳务协作帮扶协议》签约暨湖北首批 240 名赴鲁务工人员送迎仪式。图为即将赴鲁就业的湖北务工人员乘坐大巴车从黄冈出发。（新华社记者程敏摄）

Photo shows Hubei migrant workers who are about to work in Shandong leave the city of Huanggang by bus. On May 14, 2020, Hubei and Shandong provinces signed an agreement on supporting poor laborers in seeking jobs outside their hometowns and held a send-off ceremony for the first batch of 240 Hubei migrant workers leaving for Shandong by video link. (Xinhua/Cheng Min)

湖北省恩施土家族苗族自治州宣恩县对扶贫工厂（车间）采取优先复工复产、部门跟踪服务等措施，保障扶贫工厂（车间）有序组织生产销售，并适时扩展经营规模，使之成为山区农民成功就业的"稳压器"。图为 2020 年 7 月 13 日，在高罗镇龙河村一家吸纳 400 余人的扶贫工厂的车间里，就业农民在制衣生产线上劳作。（新华社发　宋文摄）

Photo shows farmers work on a garment production line at a poverty alleviation workshop in Longhe Village, Xuan'en County, Hubei Province, on July 13, 2020. Poverty alleviation factories (workshops) provide jobs for farmers in the mountainous area. (Xinhua/Song Wen)

2020年9月11日，四川省凉山彝族自治州越西县城北感恩社区的部分妇女正在接受家政服务培训。（新华社记者刘坤摄）

Women take part in a household service training at a community in Yuexi County, southwest China's Sichuan Province, on Sept. 11, 2020. (Xinhua/Liu Kun)

2017年7月22日，在江西省赣州市石城县小松镇桐江村，村民在就业扶贫车间内制鞋。（新华社记者彭昭之摄）

Villagers make shoes in a poverty alleviation workshop of Tongjiang Village, Shicheng County, east China's Jiangxi Province, on July 22, 2017. (Xinhua/Peng Zhaozhi)

2020 年 5 月 10 日拍摄的山西省岢岚县宋家沟村村民在食品加工厂包装沙棘饮料。（新华社记者曹阳摄）

Villagers pack soft drink at a plant in Songjiagou Village in Kelan County, north China's Shanxi Province, May 10, 2020. (Xinhua/Cao Yang)

2020 年 6 月 3 日，河北省深州市高古庄镇凤凰池村村民在扶贫车间做缝纫工作。（新华社记者李晓果摄）

Villagers at Fenghuangchi Village, Gaoguzhuang Town, Shenzhou City, in north China's Hebei Province are sewing in the poverty alleviation workshop, June 3, 2020. (Xinhua/Li Xiaoguo)

2018 年 7 月 5 日，山东青岛市即墨区移风店镇电商培训中心的工作人员原丽琴（前左）在指导贫困户通过网络销售农产品。（新华社发 梁孝鹏摄）

A technician helps farmers in Yifengdian Township of Qingdao City, east China's Shandong Province in selling products on an online platform, July 5, 2018. (Xinhua/Liang Xiaopeng)

2020 年 4 月 5 日，在湖北省恩施市李家河镇塘坊易地扶贫搬迁安置点的童话工艺"扶贫工厂"里，务工人员将制作好的玩具装入玩具收纳壳。（新华社发　王俊摄）

Workers make toys at a workshop of a poverty-relief relocation site at Lijiahe Township of Enshi City, central China's Hubei Province, April 5, 2020. (Xinhua/ Wang Jun)

2020 年 1 月 10 日，在黑龙江省克东县的黑龙江满艺工艺品有限公司，脱贫户杨伶俐正在制作一幅满绣作品。（新华社发　谢剑飞摄）

Photo taken on Jan. 10, 2020 shows Yang Lingli is making a Manchu embroidery at a craft company in Kedong County, northeast China's Heilongjiang Province. (Xinhua/Xie Jianfei)

甘肃省临夏回族自治州和政县依托东西部扶贫协作平台，引进鞋业、包袋、食用菌种植等企业，以扶贫车间的模式带动贫困户就近就业，助力脱贫增收。图为 2020 年 10 月 17 日，和政县一扶贫车间里，工人在包袋生产线上作业。（新华社发　史有东摄）

Photo shows villagers work on a bag production line at a poverty alleviation workshop in Hezheng County, northwest China's Gansu Province, on Oct. 17, 2020. Relying on the east-west poverty alleviation cooperation platform, Hezheng attracted enterprises in shoe, bag, and edible fungus cultivation industries. The poverty alleviation workshops employed nearby poor farmers. (Xinhua/Shi Youdong)

"楼上过日子，楼下赚票子"是来自陕西省安康市的易地扶贫搬迁一线的写照。图为 2018 年 9 月 11 日，汉滨区谭坝镇松坝社区的居民在社区的毛绒玩具厂内工作。（新华社记者邵瑞摄）

Photo shows residents of Songba Community, Ankang City, northwest China's Shaanxi Province, work in a toy factory, Sept. 11, 2018. (Xinhua/Shao Rui)

图为 2020 年 10 月 17 日，甘肃省临夏回族自治州和政县一扶贫车间里，工人在生产线上作业。（新华社发 史有东摄）

Photo taken on Oct. 17, 2020 shows people working at the production line in Hezheng County, northwest China's Gansu Province. (Xinhua/Shi Youdong)

　　2018 年 8 月 22 日，江西省万安县张春妹（左二）和丈夫许礼良（左一）拿着当地政府颁发的脱贫荣誉证书和家人一起在家门前合影。（新华社记者胡晨欢摄）

Zhang Chunmei (2nd L) and Xu Liliang, a couple from Wan'an County, east China's Jiangxi Province, take a family photo in front of their home, Aug. 22, 2018, after the family rise above poverty. (Xinhua/Hu Chenhuan)

甘肃省庆阳市镇原县新集镇吴塬村村民张小花 2013 年被确立为建档立卡贫困户。2019 年，通过项目奖补资金和政府配股等方式，张小花积极发展养兔、养羊产业，丈夫薛进张就近外出务工。2020 年 9 月，他们一家正式脱贫摘帽，成为村里最后一批脱贫户。图为张小花（右）和丈夫薛进张展示刚刚拿到的贫困户脱贫光荣证。（新华社记者陈斌摄）

Photo taken on Sept. 21, 2020 shows Zhang Xiaohua(R) and her husband Xue showing a certificate marking their farewell to poverty. The family of Zhang in Wuyuan Village, Zhenyuan County, northwest China's Gansu Province, was registered as an impoverished household in 2013. In 2019, she began raising rabbits and goats with support from the local government. Her husband Xue Jinzhang got a job not far away from home. In September 2020, the family shook off poverty, one of the last batch of households in the village that are lifted out of poverty. (Xinhua/Chen Bin)

2020 年 5 月 2 日在西藏昌都市贡觉县莫洛镇，无人机拍摄的阿旺绵羊繁育基地。（新华社记者詹彦摄）

Aerial photo taken on May 2, 2020 shows a sheep breeding base in Molo Town, Konjo County, Qamdo City of Tibet Autonomous Region. (Xinhua/Zhan Yan)

变迁·跨越

CHANGES & BEYOND

上图为 2019 年 9 月拍摄的甘肃省渭源县元古堆村村貌。下图为 2013 年 3 月拍摄的脱贫前的渭源县元古堆村一处民居。（新华社记者范培坤摄）

The upper photo, taken in September 2019, shows the scenery of Yuangudui Village, Weiyuan County of Gansu Province. The lower photo, taken in March 2013, shows a folk house of Yuangudui Village in Weiyuan County, before it was lifted out of poverty. (Xinhua/Fan Peishen)

2016 年 8 月 22 日至 24 日，中共中央总书记、国家主席、中央军委主席习近平在青海调研考察。图为 23 日上午，习近平在互助土族自治县五十镇班彦村考察时同村民合影。（新华社记者兰红光摄）

Presient Xi Jinping, also general secretary of the CPC Central Committee and chairman of the CMC, poses for a group photo with villagers in Banyan Village of Wushi Township of Huzhu Tu Autonomous County, Qinghai Province, on Aug. 23 morning, 2016, during an inspection tour in northwest China's Qinghai Province from Aug. 22 to 24, 2016. (Xinhua/Lan Hongguang)

2016 年 12 月 25 日，青海省互助土族自治县班彦村易地扶贫搬迁新村，村民吕有金（右二）和老伴在新家里照顾孙女。（新华社记者王大千摄）

On Dec. 25, 2016, Banyan Village relocated to a new village through poverty relocation program. Villager Lyu Youjin (2nd R) and his wife look after their granddaughters in the new home. (Xinhua/Wang Daqian)

2016 年 11 月 1 日无人机拍摄的青海省互助土族自治县五十镇班彦村易地扶贫搬迁新村村貌。（新华社记者吴刚摄）

The aerial photo taken on Nov. 1, 2016 shows the new village of Banyan of Wushi Township in Huzhu Tu Autonomous County, Qinghai Province. (Xinhua/Wu Gang)

中华民族传统节日农历春节来临之际，中共中央总书记、国家主席、中央军委主席习近平来到四川考察调研，看望慰问各族干部群众，向全国各族人民致以美好的新春祝福。这是 2018 年 2 月 11 日上午，习近平在凉山彝族自治州昭觉县三岔河乡三河村看望慰问全村群众。（新华社记者谢环驰摄）

Presient Xi Jinping, also general secretary of the CPC Central Committee and chairman of the CMC, meets with the villagers as he visits Sanhe Village of Sanchahe Township in Zhaojue County of Liangshan Yi Autonomous Prefecture, southwest China's Sichuan Province, on Feb. 11, 2018, during his inspection tour in Sichuan ahead of the traditional Spring Festival. (Xinhua/Xie Huanchi)

2019 年 2 月 11 日，在四川省昭觉县三河村的易地扶贫安置点，彝族群众庆祝乔迁之喜。（新华社记者江宏景摄）

eople of the Yi ethnic group celebrate their relocation to new homes at a resettlement site for poverty alleviation in Sanhe Village, Zhaojue County, southwest China's ichuan Province, on Feb. 11, 2019. (Xinhua/Jiang Hongjing)

位于大凉山腹地的四川省昭觉县三河村首批 29 户、168 人告别居住多年的土坯房，搬入易地扶贫安置点的新家。左图是 2019 年 2 月 11 日无人机拍摄的昭觉县三河村原来的土坯房。下图是 2 月 11 日无人机拍摄的三河村易地扶贫安置点。（新华社记者江宏景摄）

In the hinterland of Daliang Mountain, the first batch of 168 residents from 29 households in Sanhe Village of Zhaojue County, Sichuan Province, left the adobe houses where they had lived for many years, and moved into new homes in relocation settlements for poverty alleviation.

The aerial photo on the left, taken on Feb. 11, 2019, shows former adobe houses in Sanhe Village of Zhaojue County. The lower aerial photo taken on Feb. 11, shows the relocation settlements of Sanhe Village. (Xinhua/Jiang Hongjing)

2019 年 8 月 19 日至 22 日，中共中央总书记、国家主席、中央军委主席习近平在甘肃考察。图为 21 日上午，习近平在古浪县黄花滩生态移民区富民新村村民李应川家，关心询问李应川一家的生产生活状况。（新华社记者谢环驰摄）

Presient Xi Jinping, also general secretary of the CPC Central Committee and chairman of the CMC, visits local resident Li Yingchuan's new home at Huanghuatan Community, which is home to rural residents relocated from environmentally vulnerable and impoverished areas, in Gulang County, northwest China's Gansu Province, during his inspection tour from Aug. 19 to 22, 2019. (Xinhua/Xie Huanchi)

　　地处祁连山脚下的甘肃省古浪县是六盘山集中连片特困地区。上图为 2018 年 2 月 6 日无人机拍摄的古浪县黄羊川镇石城村原貌。下图为 2020 年 3 月 10 日无人机拍摄的石城村群众易地扶贫搬迁入住的古浪县黄花滩生态移民区绿洲生态移民小镇。（新华社记者范培坤摄）

Located at the foot of the Qilian Mountains, Gulang County in Gansu Province, is among the concentrated and contiguous areas of extreme poverty in Liupan Mountains. The upper photo, taken on Feb. 6, 2018 with a drone, shows the original layout of Shicheng Village, Huangyangchuan Township, Gulang County. The lower photo, taken on March 20, 2020 with a drone, shows the oasis town in Huanghuatan ecological resettlement zone in Gulang County, where villagers of Shicheng are relocated. (Xinhua/Fan Peishen)

　　2020 年 3 月 10 日无人机拍摄的古浪县黄花滩生态移民区富民新村全景。甘肃省武威市古浪县黄花滩生态移民区富民新村大力发展日光温室大棚蔬菜种植、肉羊养殖、林果经济等产业，累计建成种植西红柿、辣椒、西瓜等蔬果的日光温室大棚 230 座；建成养殖暖棚 2000 多座，现阶段羊存栏 1.8 万只；新栽植山楂 100 亩、桃 300 亩、李子 70 亩等经济林，通过多渠道发展脱贫致富产业，让易地扶贫搬迁的群众留得住、能就业、有收入。（新华社记者范培珅摄）

Panorama photo taken on March 10, 2020 with a drone shows Fumin New Village in the Huanghuatan ecological resettlement zone in Gulang County. The village, located in Huanghuatan ecological resettlement zone in Gulang County, Wuwei City of Gansu Province, has made huge efforts to develop industries including vegetable planting in solar greenhouses, sheep breeding. The village has accumulatively built 230 solar greenhouses for vegetables and fruits including tomato, pepper and watermelon; constructed more than 2,000 breeding greenhouses where 18,000 sheep are kept in stock. Some 100 mu (about 6.67 hectares) of hawthorn, 300 mu of peach trees, 70 mu of plum trees and other forests have been planted to develop industries through multiple channels to facilitate poverty alleviation and help relocated villagers get rich so that they can stay on, get employed and have income. (Xinhua/Fan Peishen)

图为 2015 年 2 月 14 日拍摄的甘肃省临夏回族自治州东乡族自治县布楞沟村地形景貌。（新华社发　郭得侠摄）

The photo taken on Feb. 14, 2015 shows the barren landscape of the Bulenggou Village in Dongxiang Autonomous County in Linxia Hui Autonomous Prefecture, northwest China's Gansu Province. (Xinhua/Guo Dexia)

重庆市酉阳县寇军山公路大桥。（刘前刚摄　1996 年 8 月 16 日发）

Photo published on Aug. 16, 1996 shows the Koujunshan Highway Bridge in Youyang County, Chongqing Municipality. (Xinhua/Liu Qiangang)

云南省贡山独龙族怒族自治县独龙江乡的独龙族群众在 20 世纪 50 年代刀耕火种的资料照片。（新华社发）

The Drung people engaged in slash-and-burn farming in Dulongjiang Township, Drung-Nu Autonomous County of Gongshan in southwest China's Yunnan Province in the 1950s. (Xinhua)

　　2005 年 6 月 5 日，住在四川省布拖县阿布洛哈村的且沙次干背羊过溜索。2020 年 6 月 30 日，一条 3.8 公里的通村公路建成通车了，且沙次干从家门口坐车 10 多分钟即可出村，两个小时就能到县城。（新华社发　林强摄）

File photo taken on June 5, 2005 shows a villager carrying a goat passes the Xixi River by using a cable in Abuluoha Village, Butuo County, southwest China's Sichuan Province. The construction of a road linking the village was completed on June 30, 2020. Villagers can travel to the county in two hours. (Xinhua/Lin Qiang)

　　隔江相望的傈僳族、怒族和独龙族同胞通过钢绳滑轮溜索过江。（新华社记者李玉龙摄　1984 年 6 月 5 日发）

People from the ethnic groups of Lisu, Nu and Drung cross a river through ziplines as shown in the photo published on June 5, 1984. (Xinhua/Li Yulong)

　　重庆市石柱县为打通一条从县城到长江边的出山通道，上万名农民苦干 70 天，用"蚂蚁啃骨头"的精神，硬修出了一条 23 公里长的二级公路。（刘前刚摄　1996 年 8 月 16 日发）

In Shizhu County of southwest China's Chongqing Municipality, tens of thousands of farmers worked hard for 70 days to create a passage through the mountains to connect the county seat and the bank of Yangtze River, as is portrayed in the photo published on Aug. 16, 1996. With the perseverance that parallels "ants gnawing at bones," they finished paving a 23-km secondary road. (Xinhua/Liu Qiangang)

在巴颜喀喇山海拔 4000 多米的高寒牧区，活跃着一支外科手术队伍，由青海省果洛藏族自治州上红科公社的藏族"赤脚医生"组成。图为"赤脚医生"在为儿童防疫。（新华社记者李基禄摄　1975 年 7 月 29 日发）

The photo published on July 29, 1975 shows a "barefoot doctor," or primary health care worker, preventing epidemics among children. In the alpine pastures of Bayan Har Mountains with an altitude of over 4,000 meters, works a surgical team of Tibetan "barefoot doctors" from Golog Tibetan Autonomous Prefecture, northwest China's Qinghai Province. (Xinhua/Li Jilu)

上图为 2016 年 11 月 23 日，云南省贡山独龙族怒族自治县独龙江乡独龙族群众高德生、高琼先和黎英家三口（从左到右）在中心小学新校舍前合影。（新华社记者胡超摄）下图为 1993 年高德生、高琼先和黎英在小学旧校舍前合影（资料照片）。

The upper photo was taken on Nov. 23, 2016 of Drung people Gao Desheng, Gao Qiongxian and Li Ying (L to R) in front of the new school building of the central primary school in Drung-Nu Autonomous County of Gongshan, southwest China's Yunnan Province. (Xinhua/Hu Chao) The lower photo taken in 1993 shows Gao Desheng, Gao Qiongxian and Li Ying, a family of three, at the school's old site. (file photo)

自主学习　快乐同行　健康发展

普洱市西盟佤族自治县位于云南省西南部中缅边境的大山深处，曾经是国家扶贫工作重点县。上图：2016年9月22日，西盟民族小学的孩子们在教室里上课。（新华社记者蔺以光摄）下图：20世纪50年代中期拍摄的一些孩子在土屋中读书（新华社发）。

Located deep in the mountains along the border between China and Myanmar in southwest China's Yunnan Province, the Ximeng Wa Autonomous County of Pu'er City was one of the country's most impoverished counties that are high on the poverty alleviation programs. The upper photo shows students at Ximeng ethnic primary school having a class on Sept. 22, 2016. (Xinhua/Lin Yiguang) The lower photo was taken of children reading books in a hut in the 1950s. (Xinhua)

上图：2007 年拍摄的云南省贡山独龙族怒族自治县独龙江乡迪政当村小学的学生在室外上体育课。（资料照片）下图：2016 年 11 月 23 日拍摄的孩子们在独龙江乡中心小学里打篮球。（新华社记者胡超摄）

The upper file photo, taken in 2007, shows the students of Dizhengdang Village primary school in Dulongjiang Township, Drung-Nu Autonomous County of Gongshan of southwest China's Yunnan Province taking physical education classes outdoors. (file photo) The lower photo shows children playing basketball in the central primary school in Dulongjiang Township on Nov. 23, 2016. (Xinhua/Hu Chao)

借脱贫攻坚之力，哈尼族群众正在用双手播洒脱贫致富的希望。上图为 1958 年，云南省墨江哈尼族自治县群众在县城外劳作。（墨江哈尼族自治县档案局提供）下图为 2017 年 1 月 11 日墨江哈尼族自治县那哈乡那苏村的哈尼族农妇周布书（左）、张万书在茶园里给茶树修枝整形（新华社记者胡超）。

The country's efforts in poverty alleviation have helped the Hani people shake off poverty by their own hands. The upper photo was taken of people in Mojiang Hani Autonomous County of southwest China's Yunnan Province working outside county seat in 1958. (Photo provided by the Mojiang Hani Autonomous County Archive Bureau) The lower photo was taken on Jan. 11, 2017 of Hani farmer Zhou Bushu (L) and Zhang Wanshu trimming tea trees in Nasu Village, Naha Township, Mojiang Hani Autonomous County. (Xinhua/Hu Chao)

上图为 1996 年，甘肃省宕昌县车拉乡农民徒步走出大山。（新华社记者武斌摄）

下图为 2016 年 12 月 25 日拍摄的即将开通的兰渝铁路陇南境内白龙江 3 号特大桥（右）与高速公路从山脚下蜿蜒伸出。（新华社记者陈斌摄）

The upper photo shows farmers of Chela Township of Tanchang County, Gansu Province travelling out of the mountains on foot in 1996. (Xinhua/Wu Bin)

The lower photo taken on Dec. 25, 2016 shows a bridge across the Bailong River (R) on the Lanzhou-Chongqing Railway which was to be soon put into operation and an expressway in Longnan, Gansu Province, wind their way out from the foot of the mountain. (Xinhua/Chen Bin)

左图为 2017 年 1 月 11 日拍摄的水泥公路已经从学校修通到家门口；右图为 2012 年 9 月 3 日拍摄的广西大化瑶族自治县板升乡弄勇村弄顶屯的孩子们扛着生活用具去学校。（新华社记者黄孝邦摄）

The left photo taken on Jan. 11, 2017 shows a cement road has extended to students' doorstep from school. The right photo taken on Sept. 3, 2012 shows children from the Nongyong Village of Bansheng Township, Dahua Yao Autonomous County, south China's Guangxi Zhuang Autonomous Region walk to school carrying daily necessity. (Xinhua/Huang Xiaobang)

2017 年 3 月 24 日，广西大化瑶族自治县七百弄乡弄雄村的一条屯级公路。（新华社记者黄孝邦摄）

Photo taken on March 24, 2017 shows a village road of Nongxiong Village of Qibainong Township in Dahua Yao Autonomous County, south China's Guangxi Zhuang Autonomous Region. (Xinhua/Huang Xiaobang)

　　上图为 2013 年 2 月 2 日，在云南省怒江傈僳族自治州泸水县六库镇双米地村辣子咪村民小组，一名傈僳族男子带着自行车溜索过怒江。（新华社记者蔺以光摄）下图为 2016 年 9 月 9 日拍摄的怒江傈僳族自治州大型公路跨江桥梁——通达桥。（新华社记者胡超摄）

The upper photo taken on Feb. 2, 2013 shows a man of Lisu ethnic group from Shuangmidi Village of Liuku Township is crossing the Nujiang River carrying his bike via a zipline in Lushui County of Nujiang Lisu Autonomous Prefecture, Yunnan Province. (Xinhua/Lin Yiguang)

The lower photo taken on Sept. 9, 2016 shows a highway bridge, Tongda Bridge, across a river in Nujiang Lisu Autonomous Prefecture, Yunnan Province. (Xinhua/Hu Chao)

上图为云南省贡山独龙族怒族自治县巴坡村的普学清站在新建的安居房台阶上。下图为 2017 年 5 月 25 日拍摄的普学清站在以前居住的茅草屋前。（新华社记者杨宗友摄）

The upper photo shows Pu Xueqing stands on the doorsteps of his newly-built government-subsidized house in Bapo Village of Drung-Nu Autonomous County of Gongshan, Yunnan Province. The lower photo taken on May 25, 2017 shows Pu Xueqing stands in front of his old thatched cottage. (Xinhua/Yang Zongyou)

上图为 2018 年 11 月 11 日在广西田东县思林镇龙邦村拍摄的村民和自家简陋的房屋。（思林镇党委宣传部供图）下图为 2019 年 8 月 28 日无人机拍摄的田东县思林镇易地扶贫搬迁安置点。（新华社记者曹祎铭摄）

The upper photo taken on Nov. 11, 2018 shows villagers and their run-down house in Longbang Village, Silin Township of Tiandong County, Guangxi Zhuang Autonomous Region. (photo provided by the government of Silin Township)

The lower aerial photo taken on Aug. 28, 2019 shows a poverty-relief resettlement site in Silin Township of Tiandong County, Guangxi Zhuang Autonomous Region. (Xinhua/Cao Yiming)

2018 年 3 月 29 日，无人机拍摄的云南省威信县庙沟乡扎实沟村易地搬迁房一景。（新华社记者胡超摄）

An aerial photo taken on March 29, 2018 shows the poverty-relief resettlement houses in Zhashigou Village, Miaogou Township of Weixin County, Yunnan Province. (Xinhua/Hu Chao)

上图为在尚未通路的广西大化瑶族自治县板升乡八好村八好屯，村民背着年货走山路回家（2016 年 1 月 26 日摄）。下图为 2019 年 11 月 11 日无人机拍摄的已经修通水泥路的八好村八好屯。（新华社记者黄孝邦摄）

The upper photo taken on Jan. 26, 2016 shows villagers carrying Spring Festival purchases on a mountain trail walk to their home village of Bahao in Bansheng Township, Dahua Yao Autonomous County, Guangxi Zhuang Autonomous Region. The village had no paved roads then. The lower aerial photo taken on Nov. 11, 2019 shows the Bahao Village, now accessible by cement roads. (Xinhua/Huang Xiaobang)

2017 年 1 月 24 日，河北省张北县小二台镇德胜村村民徐学海（左二）与家人合影。（新华社记者牟宇摄）

On Jan. 24, 2017, villager Xu Xuehai (2nd L) and his family in Desheng Village, Xiaoertai Township of Zhangbei County in Hebei Province take a group photo. (Xinhua/Mou Yu)

　　2018 年 4 月 22 日，在西藏林芝市派镇索松村索松客栈，拉巴卓玛（左一）和丈夫向客人推介当地的土特产。（新华社记者张汝锋摄）

Lhapa Drolma (1st L) and her husband promote local specialties to visitors on April 22, 2018, in an inn in Suosong Village, Paizhen Township, Nyingchi City, Tibet Autonomous Region. (Xinhua/Zhang Rufeng)

　　2018 年 5 月 17 日，西藏林芝市羌纳乡巴嘎村村民久米的民宿旅游园一角。（新华社记者张汝锋摄）

The photo taken on May 17, 2018 shows a corner of Jumi's home-stay garden, which is located at the Parga Village, Qabnag Township, Nyingchi City, Tibet Autonomous Region. (Xinhua/Zhang Rufeng)

　　图①为楚松村村民欧珠加措的第一代房子；图②为他的第二代房子；图③为他的第三代房子；图④为他的第四代房子。（新华社记者刘东君摄）

Photo 1 to 4 show the houses of Ngodrup Gyastso, a villager in Chusong, from the first generation to the fourth generation. (Xinhua/Liu Dongjun)

　　2018 年 9 月 16 日，位于西藏阿里地区的札达县楚鲁松杰乡楚松村，每年大雪封山时间长达半年。山坡台地上，老房、新房，"四代同堂"，仿佛中国边陲巨变的缩微影像。（新华社记者刘东君摄）

The photo taken on Sept. 16, 2018 shows the coexistence of houses of four generations on the hill where the Chusong Village, in Cosibsumgyi Township, Zanda County of Ali Prefecture, Tibet Autonomous Region, is located. The mountain is covered with snow for as long as six months of a year. The picture reflects the huge changes in China's border areas. (Xinhua/Lin Dongjun)

云南省景洪市基诺山基诺族适龄儿童的入学率和巩固率都已达 100%。上图为 1984 年拍摄的基诺山的学生在上课。（资料照片）下图为 2018 年 11 月 20 日拍摄的基诺山基诺族乡民族小学的学生在上计算机课。（新华社记者蔺以光摄）

All school-age Jino children on Jino Mountain in Jinghong City, Yunnan Province, are attending schools. The upper file photo shows students on Jino Mountain attending a class in 1984; and the lower photo taken on Nov. 20, 2018 shows students taking a computer lesson at the Ethnic Primary School in Jino Ethnic Township on Jino Mountain. (Xinhua/Lin Yiguang)

上图为 1981 年拍摄的云南省景洪市基诺山的群众在交售木耳和笋干。（资料照片）下图为 2018 年 11 月 20 日拍摄的基诺山基诺族乡巴朵村的基诺族妇女李晓慧在自己经营的农村电子商务服务站内整理货品。（新华社记者蔺以光摄）

The upper file photo shows residents of Jino Mountain in Jinghong City, Yunnan Province, selling edible fungi and bamboo shoots in 1981; and the lower photo taken on Nov. 20, 2018 shows Jino villager Li Xiaohui arranging goods at her own e-commerce center in Baduo Village of Jino Ethnic Township on Jino Mountain. (Xinhua/Lin Yiguang)

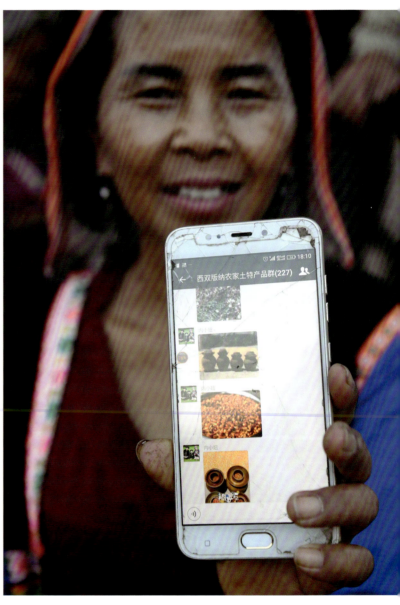

　　左图为 1984 年拍摄的云南省景洪市基诺山的几名基诺族妇女用脚踩稻穗脱粒的场景。（资料照片）右图为 2018 年 11 月 20 日拍摄的基诺山基诺族巴卡村的基诺族妇女李秀珍用手机展示她家使用微商出售土特产的微信群。（新华社记者蔺以光摄）

The left photo taken in 1984 shows Jino women in Jino Ethnic Township, Jinghong City, Yunnan Province, shelling rice ears with their feet. (file photo) The right photo taken on Nov. 20, 2018 shows Li Xiuzhen, a Jino woman in Baka Village, showing a WeChat group through which she sells local specialties. (Xinhua/Lin Yiguang)

2018 年 6 月 21 日，在河南兰考张庄村，村民在整理自家经营的民宿的客房。（新华社记者冯大鹏摄）

On June 21, 2018, a villager of Zhangzhuang in Lankao County, Henan Province, is tidying up a guest room of the family-owned home-stay hotel. (Xinhua/Feng Dapeng)

近年来，贵州省丹寨县通过推广非遗文化旅游新模式，助推脱贫增收。图为在丹寨县万达小镇，游客杨学亮（左）在吴正伟的鸟笼制作体验馆中学习手工制作鸟笼。（新华社发　吴吉斌摄）

Over the years, the Danzhai County, Guizhou Province, has popularized a new tourism model of intangible cultural heritage to promote poverty alleviation and increase income. The photo shows a visitor, Yang Xueliang (L), is learning to make a bird cage at a studio owned by Wu Zhengwei. (Xinhua/Wu Jibin)

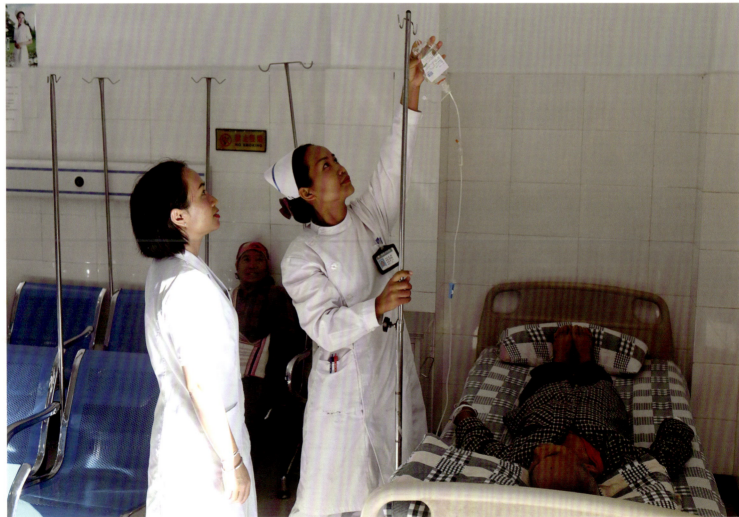

　　通过脱贫攻坚，基诺族乡参加城乡居民基本保险的村民占 99% 以上。上图为 1977 年拍摄的基诺山的基诺族医生白腊蕾（中）在户外为群众看病。（资料照片）下图为 2018 年 11 月 20 日基诺族乡卫生院的基诺族医护人员周益芳（左一）和周静（左二）在为患者输液。（新华社记者蔺以光摄）

Thanks to poverty alleviation, more than 99 percent of residents in Jino Ethnic Township have joined the rural cooperative medical insurance programme. The upper file photo taken in 1977 shows Jino doctor Bai Lalei (C) giving medical treatment to villagers on Jino Mountain; and the lower photo taken on Nov. 20, 2018 shows Jino medical workers Zhou Yifang (1st L) and Zhou Jing (2nd L) giving injection for a patient at a local hospital in Jino Ethnic Township on Jino Mountain. (Xinhua/Lin Yiguang)

上图为 2013 年 3 月脱贫前的甘肃省渭源县元古堆村的孩子们从取水点抬水。下图为 2019 年 9 月渭源县元古堆村村民在自来水龙头前接水。（新华社记者范培珅摄）

The upper photo taken in March 2013 shows children in Yuangudui Village of Weiyuan County, Gansu Province, taking water from a water point. The lower photo taken in September 2019, shows villagers of Yuangudui taking tap water. (Xinhua/Fan Peishen)

1977 年秋，陕西省榆林市补浪河女子民兵治沙连的民兵们向毛乌素沙漠进军。（资料照片 新华社发）

In the autumn of 1977, members from the women's militia sand control company of Bulang River in Yulin City, Shaanxi Province, marched into the Maowusu desert. (Xinhua/file photo)

山西省右玉县地处晋蒙交界、毛乌素沙漠边缘，近年来的脱贫攻坚中，靠着一辈辈种树改良的土壤和改善的环境，发展药材产业、兴建旅游项目，走出了一条绿色脱贫路。图为 2018 年 10 月 25 日无人机拍摄的右玉县杀虎口村村貌。（新华社记者杨晨光摄）

Youyu County of Shanxi Province is located on the edge of Maowusu desert and on the juncture of Shanxi Province and Inner Mongolia Autonomous Region. It has adopted a green approach of poverty elimination in recent years while developing the medicine material and tourism industries as generations' tree planting has ameliorated the soil and improved the environment. Aerial photo taken on Oct. 25, 2018 shows a view of Shahukou Village of Youyu County. (Xinhua/Yang Chenguang)

　　上图为 2014 年 5 月脱贫前的河南省兰考县张庄村一处民居。（新华社发）下图为 2019 年 9 月兰考县张庄村村貌和种植大棚。（新华社记者李安摄）

The upper photo taken in May 2014 shows a residential building in Zhangzhuang Village of Lankao County, Henan Province, before it shook off poverty. (Xinhua)

The lower photo taken in September 2019 shows Zhangzhuang Village of Lankao County and its greenhouses. (Xinhua/ Li An)

盐池县是宁夏首个脱贫摘帽县。图为 2019 年 5 月 28 日无人机拍摄的盐池县县城局部。（新华社记者丁洪法摄）

Yanchi County is the first county shaking off poverty in Ningxia Hui Autonomous Region. Aerial photo taken on May 28, 2019, shows part of Yanchi County. (Xinhua/Ding Hongfa)

上图为山西省闻喜县张才岭村十八坪自然村村民原来所住的窑洞（2019 年 1 月 27 日摄）。下图为 2019 年 1 月 26 日闻喜县张才岭村村民的新居"幸福小院"。（新华社记者詹彦摄）

The upper photo shows abandoned cave dwellings in Shibaping Village near Zhangcailing Administrative Village of Wenxi County, Shanxi Province. (Photo taken on Jan. 27, 2019)

The lower photo taken on Jan. 26, 2019, shows the "Courtyard of Happiness," a new home of a local in Zhangcailing Village, Wenxi County. (Xinhua/Zhan Yan)

上图为 2019 年 2 月 21 日无人机拍摄的贵州省石阡县城泉都易地扶贫搬迁小区。下图为 2019 年 2 月 20 日无人机拍摄的石阡县青阳乡露溪村沙坪组的旧居。（新华社记者杨文斌摄）

The upper aerial photo taken on Feb. 21, 2019, shows the Quandu relocation settlements in Shiqian County, Guizhou Province. The lower photo taken on Feb. 20, 2019, shows the old residence of Shaping Group of Luxi Village, Qingyang Township, Shiqian County. (Xinhua/Yang Wenbin)

上图为在广西都安瑶族自治县三只羊乡建良村龙牙屯，村民余万合在搬迁前的旧住房里生火（2017 年 10 月 11 日摄）。下图为在广西都安瑶族自治县三只羊乡可力易地扶贫搬迁安置新区，余万合在自己搬迁后的新住房厨房里打火准备做饭（2019 年 10 月 16 日摄）。一户户贫困群众离开闭塞的大山搬入新的家园，易地扶贫搬迁给当地各族群众带来了新生活。（新华社记者陆波岸摄）

Photo above taken on Oct. 11, 2017 shows Yu Wanhe making a fire in his house before being relocated. Yu used to live in Jianliang Village, Du'an Yao Autonomous County, south China's Guangxi Zhuang Autonomous Region. Photo below taken on Oct. 16, 2019 shows Yu cooking in his new kitchen after moving to a poverty-relief resettlement site. Poor people move to new homes from isolated mountainous areas. Poverty-alleviation relocation programs bring new life to local people of various ethnic groups. (Xinhua/Lu Boan)

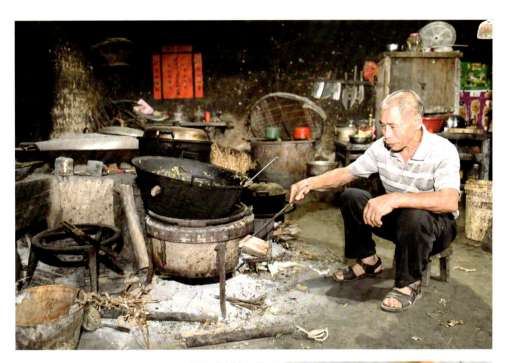

2019 年 6 月 23 日，援藏医疗队队员秦昕在甘肃省玛曲县采日玛镇为群众义诊。（新华社记者陈斌摄）

On June 23, 2019, medical aid team member Qin Xin provides free medical service for a local resident in Maqu County, Gansu Province. (Xinhua/Chen Bin)

地处帕米尔高原的热斯喀木村是新疆塔什库尔干塔吉克自治县达布达尔乡的一个小山村。上图为热斯喀木村村医发尔亚特·塔西白克骑着骆驼在山区巡诊。（资料照片）下图为 2019 年 7 月 7 日拍摄的发尔亚特·塔西白克（右三）与参加上门服务的医务人员、村民走在易地扶贫搬迁后的热斯喀木村。（新华社记者胡虎虎摄）

Located on the Pamir Plateau, Rasekam Village is a small village in Daftar Township of Taxkorgan Tajik Autonomous County, Xinjiang Uygur Autonomous Region. The upper file photo shows Falyat Tasibek, the village doctor, rides a camel on a round of visit in the mountainous areas.

The lower photo taken on July 7, 2019 shows Falyat Tasibek (3rd R) and other medical staff make a house visit at a relocated community in Rasekam Village. (Xinhua/Hu Huhu)

　　地处秦巴山区腹地的重庆市巫山县竹贤乡下庄村被称作"天坑村"。多年来，全村人凭借"不等不靠，幸福要自己造"的精神，走出了自己的一条幸福路。图为 2020 年 7 月 3 日无人机拍摄的下庄村。（新华社记者王全超摄）

Located in the Qinling-Daba mountains, the Xiazhuang Village in Zhuxian Township of Wushan County, Chongqing Municipality, was also called a village "holed up in heaven." Over the years, residents of the village have blazed a trail of happiness with the spirit of "building happiness on their own strength." The aerial photo taken on July 3, 2020 shows a view of the Xiazhuang Village. (Xinhua/Wang Quanchao)

上图为 2018 年 8 月 17 日无人机拍摄的宁夏永宁县闽宁镇原隆村。（新华社记者王鹏摄）下图为永宁县闽宁镇建设初期的状况。（资料照片）

The upper photo, taken on Aug. 17, 2018 with a drone, shows Yuanlong Village in Minning Township of Yongning County, Ningxia Hui Autonomous Region. (Xinhua/Wang Peng)

The lower file photo shows the Minning Township in the initial stage of its development.(file photo)

　　坪垭藏族乡曾经是甘肃省陇南市 25 个特困片区乡镇之一。2015 年，当地政府做出坪垭藏族乡易地扶贫搬迁重大决策，是甘肃省"十三五"时期易地扶贫搬迁工程重点建设项目。上图为武都区坪垭藏族乡腰道村木桩支撑的村内道路（2016 年 9 月 1 日摄）。下图为 2019 年 10 月 31 日无人机拍摄的武都区"新坪垭"一角。（新华社记者范培珅摄）

Pingya Ethnic Tibetan Township was one of the 25 districts and townships suffering from abject poverty in Longnan City, Gansu Province. In 2015, the local government made a major decision on the relocation of the township, which was included as one of key construction projects under Gansu's poverty-relief relocation program during the 13th Five-Year-Plan period (2016-2020). The upper photo taken on Sept. 1, 2016 shows the plank road supported by timber piles in Yaodao Village, Pingya Ethnic Tibetan Township in Wudu District. The lower photo taken with a drone on October 31, 2019 shows a corner of the "new Pingya" in Wudu District. (Xinhua/Fan Peishen)

决战决胜 中国脱贫攻坚的伟大实践　SECURING A FINAL VICTORY　China's Poverty Reduction Practice

左图为在尚未通路的广西大化瑶族自治县弄雄村弄桃屯，村民抬着准备出售的土猪走在山路上。（2016 年 12 月 8 日摄）右图为 2019 年 11 月 10 日无人机拍摄的已经通路的弄雄村弄桃屯以及周边村屯。（新华社记者黄孝邦摄）

The photo on the left, taken on Dec. 8, 2016, shows villagers carrying a hog for sale in the mountain of Nongtaotun, a hamlet in Nongxiong Village in Dahua Yao Autonomous County, Guangxi Zhuang Autonomous Region, which was not yet accessible at the time by roads.

The right photo, taken with a drone on Nov. 10, 2019, shows roads built in Nongxiong Village and its surrounding villages. (Xinhua/Huang Xiaobang)

左图为云南省会泽县马路乡的村民通过跨江人行桥前往贵州省威宁县。（2019 年 12 月 11 日摄）右图为 2013 年 3 月 7 日拍摄的会泽县火红乡的村民乘坐溜索到贵州省威宁县。（新华社记者杨文斌摄）

The photo on the left, taken on Dec. 11, 2019, shows villagers from Malu Township, Huize County, southwest China's Yunnan Province, walking on a bridge heading to Weining County in Guizhou Province. The photo on the right shows villagers of Huohong Township, Huize County, using cableway heading towards Weining County on March 7, 2013. (Xinhua/Yang Wenbin)

上图为 20 世纪末的内蒙古杭锦旗库布其沙漠。（资料照片　新华社发）下图为 2018 年 7 月 11 日无人机拍摄的库布其沙漠生态公园。（新华社记者彭源摄）

The upper file photo shows Kubuqi Desert in Hangjin Banner of Inner Mongolia Autonomous Region in the late 20th century. (Xinhua/file photo) The lower photo, taken on July 11, 2018 with a drone, shows the Kubuqi desert ecological park. (Xinhua/Peng Yuan)

2018 年 12 月 7 日拍摄的云南省西盟佤族自治县勐梭镇班母村第十村民小组老寨（上图）和新房（下图）。（新华社记者杜涓涓摄）

The upper photo taken on Dec. 7, 2018, shows the old houses of the 10th village group of the Banmu Village of Mengsuo Township in Ximeng Wa Autonomous County in Yunnan Province. The lower photo shows a new house. (Xinhua/Du Juanjuan)

上图为云南省福贡县匹河乡托坪村全景（2016年11月25日摄）。下图为2019年6月25日无人机拍摄的搬迁到怒江边的托坪村五湖易地扶贫搬迁安置点新村。（新华社记者胡超摄）

The upper photo, taken on Nov. 25, 2016, shows Tuoping village of Pihe Nu ethnic township in Fugong County of Yunnan Province. The lower photo, taken on June 25, 2019 with a drone, shows the new relocation site for poverty alleviation near the Nu River. (Xinhua/Hu Chao)

1983 年，初中毕业的吴国先来到贵州省龙里县湾滩河镇谷港小学任教，他亲自动手用木板钉成黑板，砍树制成课桌，开始给学生们上课。如今，学校已建起两层混凝土教学楼，吴国先依然坚守三尺讲台，教授一二年级所有课程，并将村里学龄前儿童接来学校免费接受学前教育。上图为 2019 年 8 月 27 日，吴国先与今年入学的部分学生在谷港小学教学楼前合影。（新华社记者杨文斌摄）下图为 20 世纪 80 年代，吴国先与学生在谷港小学老教室前合影。（资料照片）

In 1983, Wu Guoxian, a junior high school graduate, came to teach at Gugang Primary School in Wantanhe Township of Longli County, Guizhou Province. He nailed wooden boards into blackboards and cut down trees to make desks to start classes for students. Today, the school has a two-story concrete building. Wu has stuck to his post, teaching all classes in the first and second grades, and offered free preschool education to all preschoolers in the village. The upper photo, taken on Aug. 27, 2019, shows Wu taking a group photo with newly-enrolled students in front of Gugang Primary School's classroom building (Xinhua/Yang Wenbin). The lower file photo, taken in the 1980s, shows Wu and his students in front of an old classroom of Gugang Primary School.

上图为 2016 年 4 月 25 日拍摄的安徽省金寨县花石乡大湾村村民原来的住房。下图为 2019 年 5 月 18 日拍摄的大湾村易地扶贫安置点的村民新居。（新华社记者刘军喜摄）

The upper photo, taken on April 25, 2016, shows an old house in Dawan Village, Huashi Township, Jinzhai County of Anhui Province, while the lower photo, taken on May 18, 2019, shows new homes of Dawan villagers at a newly-built community for poverty alleviation relocation. (Xinhua/Liu Junxi)

经过多年的不断努力和持续攻坚，甘肃省古浪县在 2020 年年初实现整体脱贫摘帽。上图为 2016 年 4 月 21 日拍摄的定宁镇晓光村王家水小学教室旧貌。下图为 2020 年 3 月 10 日无人机拍摄的黄花滩生态移民区绿洲生态移民小镇的学校校园。（新华社记者范培坤摄）

After years of unceasing efforts, Gulang County in Gansu Province shook off poverty in early 2020. The upper photo, taken on April 21, 2016, shows an old classroom of Wangjiashui Primary School in Xiaoguang Village, Dingning Township, while the lower photo, taken with a drone on March 10, 2020, shows the new campus in the oasis ecological migration town in the Huanghuatan ecological migration zone. (Xinhua/Fan Peishen)

　　"悬崖村"是四川省凉山彝族自治州昭觉县支尔莫乡阿土列尔村的别称，其坐落在海拔 1600 米的山坳中，从山脚到山上的村庄海拔落差近千米，17 段危险的藤梯曾是其通往外界的唯一通道。2016 年 11 月，藤梯升级为由 6000 多根钢管搭建成的 2556 级钢梯。左图为在"悬崖村"曾经通往外界的唯一通道上，某色石布顺着藤梯下山上学（2016 年 9 月 30 日摄）；右图为几名游客顺着钢梯下山（2019 年 11 月 24 日摄）。（新华社记者江宏景摄）

Photo on the left shows Mou'se Shibu going down the rattan ladder to school on the only passage that once connected the "Cliff Village" to the outside world (Sept. 30, 2016); Photo on the right shows several tourists descending the mountain along the steel ladder (taken on Nov. 24, 2019). "Cliff Village" is another name for Atulieer Village, Zhaojue County, Sichuan Province. It is located in a col at 1,600 meters above sea level. In November 2016, the rattan ladder was upgraded to a 2,556-level steel ladder constructed with more than 6,000 steel pipes. (Xinhua/Jiang Hongjing)

2020 年 5 月 13 日，"悬崖村"村民沿着钢梯下山，准备搬进新家。（新华社记者江宏景摄）

On May 13, 2020, villagers from "Cliff Village" descend the mountain along the steel ladder, preparing to move into their new home. (Xinhua/Jiang Hongjing)

2020 年 5 月 12 日，四川省昭觉县阿土列尔村第一批 26 户贫困户开始搬新家，图为部分村民在山下公路边合影留念。（新华社记者江宏景摄）

On May 12, 2020, 26 poverty-stricken families in Atulie'er Village, Zhaojue County of Sichuan Province, took the lead in relocating to their new homes. The photo shows they took a group photo beside a road down the mountain. (Xinhua/Jiang Hongjing)

左图为 2011 年 12 月拍摄的脱贫前的湖南省花垣县十八洞村进村道路。（新华社发）下图为 2019 年 9 月无人机拍摄的花垣县十八洞村及进村道路。（新华社记者陈泽国摄）

The left photo, taken in December 2011, shows the road leading to the Shibadong Village of Huayuan County, Hunan Province before it threw off poverty (Xinhua). The lower photo, taken with a drone in September 2019, shows the new road and the village. (Xinhua/Chen Zeguo)

2020 年 6 月 21 日，在四川省布拖县依撒社区安置点，村民在办理确认房号手续。（新华社记者李梦馨摄）

Villagers go through formalities to confirm their new homes at a relocation site in Yisa Community, Butuo County of Sichuan Province on June 21, 2020. (Xinhua/Li Mengxin)

2016 年 5 月 25 日，黑龙江省同江市八岔村的赫哲族群众走在赫哲新居的道路上。（新华社记者王建威摄）

Hezhen people walk to their new homes in Bacha Village, Tongjiang City, Heilongjiang Province, May 25, 2016. (Xinhua/Wang Jianwei)

上图为 2020 年 6 月 27 日,四川省布拖县阿布洛哈村村民且沙次干、阿达么日杂夫妇俩在阿布洛哈村 3 组老屋土坯房前留影。下图为 2020 年 6 月 30 日,且沙次干一家人在集中安置点新居前留影。(新华社记者江宏景摄)

The upper photo shows a couple taking a photo as a souvenir in front of their old house in Abuluoha Village, Butuo County of Sichuan Province on June 27, 2020. The lower photo shows the couple and their family in front of their new home in a centralized settlement on June 30, 2020. (Xinhua/ Jiang Hongjing)

2020 年 6 月 2 日，四川省金阳县 14 个高山乡镇、38 个贫困村的 1199 户、6582 人搬迁至千户彝寨——易地扶贫搬迁东山社区集中安置点。上图为 2019 年 11 月 1 日拍摄的热柯觉乡贫困户的老房子。下图为 2020 年 6 月 2 日拍摄的易地扶贫搬迁东山社区集中安置点一角。（新华社记者江宏景摄）

Some 6,582 people from 1,199 households in 38 poor villages under 14 mountainous townships in the county of Jinyang, Sichuan Province, move to the Dongshan Community relocation site on June 2, 2020. The upper photo, taken on Nov. 1, 2019, shows the old houses of poor villagers in Rekejue Township. The lower photo, taken on June 2, 2020, shows the villagers' new homes in Dongshan Community, built under the county's poverty alleviation relocation program. (Xinhua/Jiang Hongjing)

甘肃省东乡族自治县属于"三区三州"深度贫困地区，堪称"贫中之贫，困中之困"。上图为2020年4月24日无人机拍摄的县城南区易地扶贫搬迁安置小区。下图为2019年3月5日拍摄的龙泉镇苏黑村。（新华社记者范培珅摄）

Dongxiang Autonomous County in Gansu Province is a severely impoverished area. The upper photo, taken with a drone in April 24, 2020, shows a poverty-relief relocation site in the south of the county. The lower photo, taken on March 5, 2019, shows a scene of Suhei Village, Longquan Township. (Xinhua/Fan Peishen)

2020 年年初，云南省正式宣告拉祜族等 9 个"直过民族"和人口较少民族实现整族脱贫，历史性告别绝对贫困。上图为勐海县曼班三队村村民搬迁前居住的茅草房。（资料照片）下图为 2020 年 4 月 9 日拍摄的曼班三队村容村貌。（新华社记者胡超摄）

In early 2020, Yunnan Province officially announced that nine ethnic groups with a small population, including Lahu ethnic minority, were lifted out of poverty as a whole, in a historic farewell to absolute poverty. The upper file photo shows thatched houses in Menghai County, Yunnan Province, where villagers of the Manbansandui hamlet used to live. The lower photo, taken on April 9, 2020, shows the new look of Manbansandui. (Xinhua/Hu Chao)

新疆策勒县南依昆仑山脉，北靠塔克拉玛干沙漠。长期以来，当地面临着水资源短缺和时空分布不均等难题。在脱贫攻坚进程中，策勒县持续推进改水民工程，保障城乡居民饮水安全。策勒县供水总厂工程总投入 3 亿多元，于 2019 年 9 月正式通水，覆盖策勒县城区、四个乡镇及易地搬迁区的生活用水，供水能力约 3.5 万立方米。图为 2020 年 9 月 20 日无人机拍摄的新疆策勒县供水总厂应急水库。（新华社记者胡虎虎摄）

Photo shows an emergency reservoir for a water plant in Qira County, Xinjiang Uygur Autonomous Region, on Sept. 20, 2020. The county is adjacent to the Kunlu Mountains in the south and the Taklimakan Desert in the north. For a long time, the area faced water shortage. With a total investment of over 300 million yuan, t county's water supply plant was officially opened in September 2019, providing water for the urban area as well as four townships and resettlement sites, with a da capacity of 35,000 cubic meters. (Xinhua/Hu Huhu)

在脱贫攻坚关键之年，伽师县城乡饮水安全工程近期通水。这个国家级深度贫困县的 47 万群众，终于彻底告别喝涝坝水、苦咸水的历史，喝上了"健康水""幸福水"。2020 年 6 月 8 日，在新疆喀什地区城乡供水总水厂，工作人员检查清水池工作情况。（新华社记者赵戈摄）

Photo shows staff inspecting the clean water tank at the Urban and Rural Water Supply Plant in Kashgar, Xinjiang Uygur Autonomous Region on June 8, 2020. In the critical year of poverty alleviation, the water conservancy project ensuring safe drinking water in urban and rural areas has started operation recently in Jiashi County. The 470,000 people in this state-level deeply impoverished county finally bid farewell to the history of drinking water from flooding dams and brackish water and started to drink "healthy water" and "happy water." (Xinhua/Zhao Ge)

2020 年 3 月 26 日，广西百色市隆林各族自治县新州镇岩楼村即将离任的驻村第一书记黄海棠在查看村民家门口即将通水的水龙头。（新华社记者向志强摄）

Photo taken on March 26, 2020, shows Huang Haitang, the outgoing first secretary of Yanlou Village, Longlin County, Guangxi Zhuang Autonomous Region, checks the water faucet that was about to be opened at the door of a villager's house. (Xinhua/Xiang Zhiqiang)

墨玉县曾经是国家脱贫攻坚"三区三州"重点县，新疆 22 个深度贫困县之一。截至 2019 年 11 月 1 日，墨玉县最后一批建档立卡贫困户全部通水。图为 2019 年 11 月 21 日，在和田地区墨玉县东西联合水厂，工作人员在检查设备运行情况。（新华社记者赵戈摄）

Photo shows a worker checks the operation of equipment at the East-West Joint Water Plant in Moyu County, Xinjiang Uygur Autonomous Region on Nov. 21, 2019. Moyu was a key county in China's poverty alleviation, and one of Xinjiang's 22 counties hit by deep poverty. As of Nov. 1, 2019, all registered impoverished households in Moyu County have been supplied with tap water. (Xinhua/ Zhao Ge)

　　韦小妹家曾住在位于千米山坳之上的村寨，村寨不通水、不通路、不通电，环境险恶，村民生活极其贫困。在当地政府的帮助下，韦小妹一家搬迁到了山下的马路边生活，条件大为改善。图为在广西凌云县伶站瑶族乡浩坤村，14 岁的韦小妹用台灯"照亮"7 年前在煤油灯下学习的哥哥韦富喜。（左图 2017 年 5 月 13 日摄，右图 2010 年 5 月 14 日摄　新华社记者黄孝邦摄）

Wei Xiaomei, a 14-year-old girl, uses a lamp to "illuminate" her brother Wei Fuxi, who studied under a kerosene lamp seven years ago, in Haokun Village, Lingyun County, south China's Guangxi Zhuang Autonomous Region. (Left: taken on May 13, 2017. Right: taken on May 14, 2010) Wei's family used to live in a village above a high mountain, with no access to water, roads or electricity. The environment was dangerous and the villagers lived in extreme poverty. With the help of the local government, Wei's family moved down the mountain to live along the road, where conditions improved greatly. (Xinhua/Huang Xiaobang)

　　2018 年以来，郭加新村陆续迎来 9 个高海拔县（区）的建档立卡贫困户 351 户。新村通水、通电、通路、通网络，搬迁村民从事蔬菜种植、牛羊养殖、苗圃管理等工作，居住和生活条件有了明显改善。图为 2020 年 9 月 4 日，西藏日喀则市桑珠孜区郭加新村街道上安装的太阳能节能灯。（新华社发　索朗罗布摄）

Photo shows solar energy-saving lamps installed on a street in Guojia New Village, Xigaze City in southwest China's Tibet Autonomous Region, on Sept. 4, 2020. Since 2018, Guojia New Village has welcomed 351 registered impoverished households in nine high-altitude counties (districts). The new village has access to water, electricity, roads and networks, and relocated villagers have been engaged in vegetable cultivation, cattle and sheep breeding, and nursery management. (Xinhua/Sonam Norbu)

云南省大理白族自治州洱源县在建档立卡贫困户数超过 50 户的 23 个行政村和 17 个贫困村推动基础设施建设，联通贫困村和周边城镇，打牢贫困村的发展基础。图为 2016 年 12 月 4 日，在云南省洱源县牛街乡福田村彝族北组，电力施工人员在架设电线。（新华社记者李琰摄）

..oto shows electric power construction workers set up electric wires in Futian Village, Eryuan County, southwest China's Yunnan Province on Dec. 4, 2016. Eryuan ..ounty has promoted infrastructure construction in 23 administrative villages and 17 impoverished villages with more than 50 impoverished households, connecting the ..poverished villages with neighboring towns, and laying a solid foundation for their development. (Xinhua/Li Yan)

克日泽洼村地处边远高寒牧区，平均海..超过 4100 米，自然条件复杂，是理塘县最..一个没有通电的村庄。随着精准扶贫政策的..进，克日泽洼村将会并入国家电网，接受..一供电。图为 2019 年 10 月 18 日在四川..甘孜藏族自治州理塘县禾尼乡克日泽洼村..摄的建好的电线杆。（新华社发　唐文豪摄）

..oto shows a wire pole built in Kerizewa Village, ..tang County, southwest China's Sichuan ..ovince, on Oct. 18, 2019. Kerizewa Village is ..cated in the remote alpine pastoral area, with ..mplicated natural conditions and an average ..titude of more than 4,100 meters. It is the ..st village without electricity in Litang County. ..inhua/Tang Wenhao)

　　金城江区创新实施"基层党建＋互联网＋贫困村"的"农家饭票"扶贫新模式，打通线上线下两个市场，形成群众脱贫致富、基层党组织巩固的"双赢"格局。图为 2017 年 12 月 7 日，一位游客在广西河池市金城江区六甲镇坡维村木律屯农家饭票点扫码准备就餐。（新华社记者周华摄）

Photo taken on Dec. 7, 2017 shows a tourist scanning the QR code to order meals at a local farmhouse in Powei Village, Liujia Town, Jinchengjiang District, Hechi City, Guangxi Zhuang Autonomous Region. Jinchengjiang District has innovated and implemented a new poverty alleviation model, in which internet has linked Party building activities at the primary level with poverty alleviation in villages. Through the online and offline markets, impoverished people have been lifted out of poverty, and the Party organizations at the primary level have consolidated. (Xinhua/Zhou Hua)

　　2015 年，郭晨慧从北京回乡创业，将家乡的优质土豆"搬上"互联网。她以"实体＋电商"的经营模式，逐渐建立起了集土豆种植、加工、互联网销售、民宿旅游为一体的多元产业形态。在发展自身的同时，郭晨慧积极吸纳当地的贫困户参与到土豆产业中来，带动他们脱贫致富。图为 2020 年 3 月 26 日，在内蒙古乌兰察布市察右后旗，郭晨慧利用网络直播的方式销售马铃薯。（新华社记者彭源摄）

Photo taken on March 26, 2020 shows Guo Chenhui selling potatoes by live streaming in Ulanqab city, north China's Inner Mongolia Autonomous Region. In 2015, Guo returned to her hometown from Beijing to start business, selling online high-quality potatoes grown in her hometown. While developing the business herself, Guo also hired local households in poverty to participate in the potato industry and help them out of poverty. (Xinhua/Peng Yuan)

　　2008年，罗翠美从浙江返乡创业。2015年，她创办绿色生态种养合作社，通过"合作社＋农户"的经营模式带动当地群众脱贫增收。目前，罗翠美的电商公司在当地吸纳150多人就业，其中贫困户100多人。2020年5月8日，罗翠美（右）与工作人员通过手机直播平台推销五彩糯米饭。（新华社记者曹祎铭摄）

Photo taken on May 8, 2020 shows Luo Cuimei (R) and her staffs sell colorful glutinous rice through livestreaming. In 2008, Luo returned home from Zhejiang Province to start her own business. In 2015, she set up a green ecological farming cooperative to lift the local people out of poverty and increase their income. At present, Luo's e-commerce company has employed more than 150 local residents, among whom over 100 are from poor households. (Xinhua/Cao Yiming)

2020 年 5 月 7 日无人机拍摄的吉林省和龙市"金达莱"民俗村。（新华社记者许畅摄）

The photo, taken with a drone on May 7, 2020, shows the "Jindalai" folk customs village in Helong City, Jilin Province. (Xinhua/Xu Chang)

第四部分

PART IV

拼搏 · 奉献

ENDEAVOR & DEDICATION

致富不致富，关键看干部。在脱贫攻坚战场上，基层干部在宣讲扶贫政策、整合扶贫资源、分配扶贫资金、推动扶贫项目落实等方面具有关键作用。

——2016 年 7 月 20 日，习近平在东西部扶贫协作座谈会上的讲话

贫困群众既是脱贫攻坚的对象，更是脱贫致富的主体。要加强扶贫同扶志、扶智相结合，激发贫困群众积极性和主动性，激励和引导他们靠自己的努力改变命运，使脱贫具有可持续的内生动力。

——2018 年 2 月 12 日，习近平在打好精准脱贫攻坚战座谈会上的讲话

The key to getting rich depends on cadres. In the fight against poverty, officials working at the primary levels play a key role in publicizing poverty-alleviation policies, integrating poverty-alleviation resources, allocating funds for poverty alleviation and promoting the implementation of poverty-alleviation projects.

—Xi Jinping makes the remarks at a symposium on poverty alleviation cooperation between the east and the west on July 20, 2016.

The poor are not only the target of poverty alleviation, but also the ones taking the initiative to shake off poverty and become rich. We should help the poor access education and build aspirations, and stimulate their enthusiasm and initiative, motivate and guide them in their efforts to change their destiny through hard work. Through these endeavors, our fight against poverty gains traction from the sustainable motivation of the people.

—Xi Jinping makes the remarks at a symposium on targeted poverty elimination on Feb. 12, 2018.

　　2017 年 6 月 21 日至 23 日，中共中央总书记、国家主席、中央军委主席习近平在山西考察。图为 21 日下午，习近平在岢岚县赵家洼村特困户刘福有家中察看扶贫手册。（新华社记者庞兴雷摄）

Present Xi Jinping, also general secretary of the CPC Central Committee and chairman of the CMC, checks the family poverty relief information pamphlet while visiting the poverty-stricken family of Liu Fuyou in Zhaojiawa Village of Kelan County in north China's Shanxi Province, during his inspection tour from June 21 to 23, 2017. (Xinhua/Pang Xinglei)

　　山西省岢岚县地处吕梁山集中连片特困地区，全县贫困人口主要集中在偏小穷陋村庄。上图：2018 年 2 月 15 日无人机拍摄的岢岚县广惠园新村一角。（新华社记者詹彦摄）下图：2017 年 9 月 19 日在岢岚县赵家洼村，刘福有和妻子杨娥子在院子里干活。（资料照片）

The Kelan County is located in a centralized contiguous poor area of Lyuliang Mountains in north China's Shanxi Province. Most of the county's impoverished people live in small destitute villages. The upper photo taken on Feb. 15, 2018 by a drone shows a corner of the new village of Guanghuiyuan in Kelan County. (Xinhua/Zhan Yan)

The lower file photo taken on Sept. 19, 2017 shows Liu Fuyou and his wife Yang Ezi doing chores in their yard in Zhaojiawa Village of Kelan County. (file photo)

2020 年 4 月 20 日至 23 日，中共中央总书记、国家主席、中央军委主席习近平在陕西考察。图为 4 月 20 日，习近平在商洛市柞水县小岭镇金米村培训中心，了解该村发展木耳产业的情况。（新华社记者谢环驰摄）

Xi Jinping learns about development of the black fungus industry at a training center in Jinmi Village of Xiaoling Township in Zhashui County, Shangluo City, northwest China's Shaanxi Province, April 20, 2020. Xi inspected Shaanxi Province from April 20 to 23. (Xinhua/Xie Huanchi)

2019年4月21日无人机拍摄的陕西省柞水县小岭镇金米村的地栽木耳。（新华社记者陈昌奇摄）

The photo taken by a drone on April 21, 2019 shows an agaric farm in Jinmi Village, Xiaoling Township, Zhashui County in northwest China's Shaanxi Province. (Xinhua/Chen Changqi)

　　河北农业大学教授 李保国 ，始终奋战在科技兴农、脱贫攻坚和教书育人第一线，荣获"全国先进工作者"称号，2016年去世后，被追授"全国优秀共产党员""全国脱贫攻坚模范""时代楷模"称号。2018年12月18日，党中央、国务院授予他"改革先锋"称号，颁授改革先锋奖章，并获评开创山区扶贫新路的"太行山愚公"。2019年9月17日，国家主席习近平签署主席令，授予他"人民楷模"国家荣誉称号。图为2016年1月27日他（前左）在河北省内丘县岗底村向村民讲解果树修剪知识。（新华社记者朱旭东摄）

Li Baoguo, a late professor with Hebei Agricultural University, had worked hard in the front line of promoting agriculture through science and technology, helping the poor and imparting knowledge. He was awarded the title of "National Advanced Worker." After his death in 2016, he was posthumously awarded the titles of "National Excellent CPC Member," "National Role Model for Poverty Alleviation" and "Role Model of the Times." On Dec. 18, 2018, Li Baoguo was conferred the title and medal of "Vanguard of Reform" by the CPC Central Committee and the State Council. He was honored as "Yu Gong of Taihang Mountains," for creating a new road for poverty alleviation in mountain areas. On Sept. 17, 2019, President Xi Jinping signed a presidential decree to confer him the national honorary title of "People's Role Model." Li Baoguo (Front L) tells villagers how to prune fruit trees in Gangdi Village, Neiqiu County, Hebei Province on Jan. 27, 2016. (Xinhua/Zhu Xudong)

2019 年 6 月 18 日，广西乐业县新化镇百坭村第一书记 黄文秀 回探望重病的父亲后，深夜冒雨奔向受灾群众，不幸遭遇山洪，生命远定格在扶贫路上的 30 岁。中共中央宣传部追授她"时代楷模"称；2019 年，中共中央追授她"全国优秀共产党员"称号；2021 年，黄文秀 被授予"全国脱贫攻坚楷模"荣誉称号；中共中央授予 黄文秀七一勋章"。上图为她的扶贫日记，里面记载着村里的"贫困户家庭布图"及入户走访了解到的内容。（新华社记者徐海涛摄）下图为她外村考察养蜂产业的资料照片（新华社发 乐业县宣传部供图）。

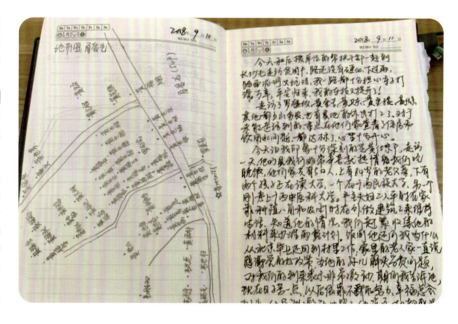

uang Wenxiu, first Party secretary of Baini Village of Xinhua Township in ye County of south China's Guangxi Zhuang Autonomous Region, died 30 on the way to visit households suffering from mountain torrents after siting her sick father on June 18, 2019. The Publicity Department of the entral Committee of the CPC awarded Huang Wenxiu the title of "Role odel of the Times." In 2019, she was awarded posthumously the title "National Outstanding Party Member" by the CPC Central Committee. 2021, Huang Wenxiu was honored as "National Role Model in Fighting overty." In 2021, the CPC Central Committee conferred on her the July 1 edal, the Party's highest honor. The upper photo shows Huang Wenxiu's overty alleviation diary, which records the "Household Distribution Map "and tails she learned from home visits. (Xinhua/Xu Haitao) The lower file photo ows Huang visiting the beekeeping industry in another village. (Xinhua/ hoto provided by Publicity Department of Leye County)

　　2016 年 4 月 12 日，贵州省晴隆县委书记、46 岁的苗族汉子姜仕坤倒在了脱贫攻坚的路上。在贫瘠的土地上破局开路、耕耘坚守，姜仕坤的忠诚与担当有如熊熊火焰照亮了 32 万晴隆人民脱贫攻坚的道路。2016 年，姜仕坤被追授"全国脱贫攻坚模范"称号；2018 年，姜仕坤被追授"全国优秀共产党员"称号；2021 年，姜仕坤被授予"全国脱贫攻坚楷模"荣誉称号。图为 2016 年 3 月 8 日，他（左三）在大田乡走访贫困户。（新华社发）

On April 12, 2016, Jiang, 46, and a man of Miao nationality, died at his post. His loyalty and responsibility have inspired 320,000 local people to throw off poverty. In 2016, he was posthumously awarded the titles of "National Role Model for Poverty Alleviation." In 2018, he was awarded posthumously the title of "National Outstanding Party Member" by the CPC Central Committee. In 2021, Jiang Shikun was honored as "National Role Model in Fighting Poverty." Jiang Shikun (3rd L), Party secretary of Qinglong County in Guizhou Province, visits impoverished households in Datian Township on March 8, 2016. (Xinhua)

　　甘肃省舟曲县扶贫办副主任张小娟被追授"全国三八红旗手""全国脱贫攻坚模范"称号；2020年，中共中央追授张小娟"全国优秀共产党员"称号；2021年，张小娟被授予"全国脱贫攻坚楷模"荣誉称号。图为2018年4月拍摄的她（右二）在下乡时向群众了解情况。（新华社发）

Zhang Xiaojuan (2nd R) chats with villagers in April 2018. Zhang, deputy director of the poverty alleviation office of Zhouqu County, Gansu Province, was posthumously awarded the honorary titles of "National March 8 Woman Pace-setter" and "National Poverty Relief Role Model." In 2020, she was awarded posthumously the title of "National Outstanding Party Member" by the CPC Central Committee. In 2021, Zhang Xiaojuan was honored as "National Role Model in Fighting Poverty." (Xinhua)

　　16 年前，重庆市巫山县下庄村党支部书记毛相林率领 100 多名下庄村民，硬是用双手在山中凿出了一条 8 公里长的公路。接着，毛相林和村民们不等不靠，敢想敢干，决战贫困，续写"愚公移山"新篇。2015 年，下庄村完成整村脱贫。2020 年 10 月，毛相林荣获全国脱贫攻坚奖，11 月，中共中央宣传部授予毛相林"时代楷模"称号；2021 年，毛相林被授予"全国脱贫攻坚楷模"荣誉称号和"全国优秀共产党员"称号。图为 2020 年 7 月 3 日拍摄的下庄村通往外界的公路。（新华社记者王全超摄）

Photo taken on July 3, 2020 shows the road from Xiazhuang Village to the outside world. Sixteen years ago, Mao Xianglin, the secretary of Communist Party of China (CPC) branch of Xiazhuang Village in Wushan County, southwest China's Chongqing Municipality, led more than 100 villagers to dig out an 8-km-long road in the mountainous area. In 2015, the whole village shook off poverty. In October 2020, Mao was granted the National Award of Poverty Alleviation. In 2021, Mao Xianglin was honored as "National Role Model in Fighting Poverty" and "National Excellent CPC Member." (Xinhua/Wang Quanchao)

2020 年 7 月 3 日在下庄村的毛相林。（新华社记者王全超摄）

Photo taken on July 3, 2020 shows Mao Xianglin in Xiazhuang Village. (Xinhua/Wang Quanchao)

参与修路的下庄村村民在悬崖峭壁上打炮眼。（新华社发　资料照片）

File photo shows villagers in Xiazhuang Village who took part in the road construction drill holes on the cliffs. (Xinhua)

革命老区炎陵地处全国 14 个集中连片特困地区之一的罗霄山片区。2011年 黄诗燕 担任炎陵县委书记以来，用九年如一日的坚守、敢啃"硬骨头"的担当、一心为民的情怀，带领炎陵成功脱贫，自己却因连续多日超负荷工作，于 2019 年 11 月 29 日突发心脏病不幸离世，献出了 56 岁的生命。2020 年 10 月，黄诗燕 被追授"全国脱贫攻坚模范"称号；2020 年 11 月，中共中央宣传部授予他"时代楷模"称号；2021 年 2 月，被中共中央、国务院授予"全国脱贫攻坚先进个人"称号；6 月，被中共中央授予"全国优秀共产党员"称号。图为 2016 年 4 月 6 日他（右）在湖南炎陵县大坑村（今大源村）走访贫困户。（新华社发）

Yanling, an old revolutionary base, sits in the Luoxiao mountain area, one of China's 14 contiguous poverty-stricken areas. Since serving as the Party secretary of Yanling County, in 2011, Huang Shiyan had worked hard over 9 years to lead the county out of poverty. He died of a heart attack at the age of 56 on Nov. 29, 2019, due to overwork for days. In October 2020, He was honored as "National Model in Fighting Poverty." In November 2020, The Publicity Department of the Central Committee of the CPC awarded him the title of "Role Model of the Times." He was awarded as "National Advanced Individual in Poverty Alleviation" by the the Central Committee of the CPC and State Council in February 2021 and "National Excellent CPC Member" by the Central Committee of the CPC in June 2021. The photo shows that Huang Shiyan (R) visits poor households in Dayuan Village, Yanling County, Hunan Province, April 6, 2016. (Xinhua)

2018 年 8 月 11 日，贵州省遵义市播州区团结村老支书黄大发沿着修建在绝壁上的"大发渠"巡查。2017 年，中共中央宣传部授予黄大发"时代楷模"称号；2020 年，黄大发被表彰为 2020 年全国劳动模范；2021 年，中共中央授予黄大发"七一勋章"。（新华社记者刘续摄）

Huang Dafa, Party secretary of Tuanjie Village in Bozhou District of Zunyi City, Guizhou Province, patrols the "Dafa Irrigation Ditch" built on the cliff, Aug. 11, 2018. In 2017, the Publicity Department of the Central Committee of the CPC awarded Huang Dafa the title of "Role Model of the Times." In 2020, Huang Dafa was awarded the title of "National Role Model Worker." In 2021, the CPC Central Committee bestowed upon Huang the July 1 Medal, the Party's highest honor. (Xinhua/Liu Xu)

四川省江油市小坝村原党支部书记青方华 24 岁时背着炸药上山修路。（翻拍资料照片 新华社发）路通了，又带领村民们种木耳、育香菇、养蜜蜂，想尽办法为村民寻找致富门路。2016 年 12 月，在走访贫困户的路上，他乘坐的车不幸坠崖，为扶贫献出了 48 岁的年轻生命。

The file photo shows 24-year-old Qing Fanghua, former Party secretary of Xiaoba Village in Jiangyou City, Sichuan Province, carrying explosives to build a road in a mountain. (Xinhua) After the road was built, Qing led the villagers to plant fungus, cultivate mushrooms and raise bees to acquire wealth. In December 2016, on the way to visit the poor villagers, Qing's car fell off a cliff. He died at the age of 48 for poverty relief.

四川乐山市公路管理局工作人员在公路管理局原党委书记、局长王川的办公室整理书籍和文件（2017 年 2 月 13 日摄）。王川在实地勘察小凉山精准扶贫交通项目时，突遇山岩崩塌，与其他 6 位同事殉职，年仅 53 岁。（新华社记者刘坤摄）

A staff member of the highway administration of Leshan City, Sichuan Province, sorts books and documents in the office of Wang Chuan, former Party secretary and director of the administration, Feb. 13, 2017. Wang, 53, died with six colleagues in a sudden rock collapse when he made a field trip to targeted poverty relief transportation projects in Xiaoliangshan region. (Xinhua/Liu Kun)

2014 年，福建省委组织部干部曾守福走进福建省宁德市下党乡下党村，履行驻村第一书记的职责——驻村帮扶，实施精准扶贫。2015 年下党村入选第一批"全国乡村旅游扶贫试点村"，村民人均纯收入达 9000 多元，实现收入翻番。图为 2016 年 10 月 11 日，曾守福（左）和同事在当地茶厂查看茶叶品质。（新华社记者林善传摄）

Photo shows Zeng Shoufu (L) and his colleagues check the quality of tea in the local tea factory in Ningde City, east China's Fujian Province, Oct. 11, 2016. Zeng, an official from the provincial organization department, came to Xiadang Village in 2014 to help with poverty alleviation. In 2015, the village was selected as the first group of pilot villages for tourism-oriented poverty reduction, and its per capita income reached 9,000 yuan, doubling the income of the previous year. (Xinhua/Lin Shanchuan)

　　2018 年 1 月 30 日，国家电网四川公司派驻凉山州喜德县光明镇阿吼村的第一书记王小兵在介绍政府出资修建的易地扶贫搬迁房。（新华社记者肖林摄）

Dispatched by the State Grid Sichuan Company, Wang Xiaobing, first Party secretary to Ahou Village, introduces the government-funded houses for relocated residents in Ahou Village, Xide County, southwest China's Sichuan Province, on Jan. 30, 2018. (Xinhua/Xiao Lin)

2020 年 6 月 3 日，山西省兴县南通村第一书记李翠叶（中）和村干部开会探讨基础设施建设问题。（新华社记者曹阳摄）

Li Cuiye (middle), first Party secretary to Nantong Village, discusses infrastructure construction with village cadres in Xingxian County, north China's Shanxi Province, on June 3, 2020. (Xinhua/Cao Yang)

脱贫攻坚战打响以来，镇赉县将产业扶贫作为精准脱贫的治本之策，积极围绕当地资源开发脱贫项目。当地在不适宜种植传统作物的地块，推广经济作物种植；依托河湖连通工程，施行荒地改水田扩大种植规模；利用各家零散闲置土地，实施庭院经济促进农民增收。图为2020年8月12日，在吉林省白城市镇赉县东屏镇白音河村，驻村第一书记朱志宇（右）查看荒地改水田扶贫产业项目的水稻长势。（新华社记者张楠摄）

Photo shows Zhu Zhiyu (R), first Party secretary to Baiyinhe Village, checks the rice growth in Zhenlai County, northeast China's Jilin Province on Aug. 12, 2020. The local government has promoted the cultivation of cash crops in plots that are not suitable for traditional crops, transformed the wastelands into paddy fields, utilizing a river-lake connection project, increase farmers' income. (Xinhua/Zhang Nan)

2015年3月，当时在贵州省剑河县烟草局工作的杨精泽被选派前往剑河县南明镇台沙村任"第一书记"。五年多来，向上级部门跑资金、拿项目、为留守儿童申请助学金补助，完善村里基础设施建设，村民们都亲切地叫他"跑腿干部"。 如今，整村脱贫的台沙村，杨精泽带领村民们探索出了一条"生态脱贫，绿色发展"的精准脱贫之路。他个人先后获得了"全州优秀共产党员""贵州省五一劳动奖章"和"全国民族团结进步模范个人"等多项荣誉。图为2020年6月29日，杨精泽（中）与村干部在台沙村讨论稻田养鱼注意事项。（新华社记者杨文斌摄）

Yang Jingze, the first Party secretary in Taisha Village in southwest China's Guizhou Province, discusses with other village officials on fish-farming in the paddle field, June 29, 2020. Yang, an official with the tobacco monopoly bureau in Jianhe County, has received several local honors for his excellent work in helping with poverty reduction, improving infrastructure and livelihood of left-behind children. (Xinhua/Yang Wenbin)

　　2017年8月李义成主动申请来到位于桂黔交界的大苗山深处广西融水苗族自治县杆洞乡尧告村担任脱贫攻坚工作队员。他和队友们从建设基础设施、发展特色脱贫产业和推进文化旅游等方面入手，积极开展各项工作。2019年，尧告村实现整体脱贫摘帽。图为2020年4月26日，李义成在尧告村高山天然牧场了解牛的长势。（新华社记者黄孝邦摄）

Li Yicheng voluntarily applied to work in Yaogao Village as a poverty alleviation team member in August 2017. Li and his colleagues have worked to improve local infrastructure, develop poverty alleviation industries with local characteristics, and promote cultural tourism. The village was lifted out of poverty in 2019. Li Yicheng learns about the growth of cattle in the high mountain natural pasture of Yaogao Village on April 26, 2020. (Xinhua/Huang Xiaobang)

　　黄河岸边的山西省永和县奇奇里村，曾经是既穷又偏的贫困村。2017年年底，奇奇里村整村脱贫。发生在奇奇里村的奇迹，离不开驻村第一书记郭若桥的努力。图为2017年10月28日郭若桥（左）在修整松动的影像展板。（新华社记者曹阳摄）

In late 2017, Qiqili Village, once a poor remote village along the Yellow River, shook off poverty. The miracle was inseparable from the efforts of Guo Ruoqiao, the village's first Party secretary. The photo shows Guo (L) repairing a video display board in the village in Yonghe County, Shanxi Province, Oct. 28, 2017. (Xinhua/Cao Yang)

2020 年 9 月 1 日，在陕西省洛南县中国邮政扶贫干部试验田里，中国邮政扶贫干部、洛南县副县长杨明（右）和辣椒专家郭永亮查看朝天椒的长势。（新华社记者李一博摄）

Yang Ming (right), a poverty alleviation cadre of China Post and deputy head of Luonan County, and Guo Yongliang, a pepper expert, check the growth of peppers in the experimental field in Luonan County, Shaanxi Province, Sept. 1, 2020. (Xinhua/Li Yibo)

2017 年，王华从中央编办来到定点帮扶的化德县，担任白音特拉村驻村第一书记。图为 2020 年 8 月 18 日，内蒙古乌兰察布市化德县白音特拉村驻村第一书记王华（左）在白音特拉村村民张丽端（右）家中向夫妻二人询问生活近况。（新华社记者彭源摄）

Wang Hua (left) asks Zhang Liduan (right), a local villager, about the family's recent life, Aug. 18, 2020. Wang, an official with a department of the CPC Central Committee came to serve as the first Party secretary of Bayintal Village in Inner Mongolia Autonomous Region in 2017. (Xinhua/Peng Yuan)

2019 年，黑龙江省饶河县西林子乡小南河村入选第一批全国乡村旅游重点村名单。从 2016 年开始开展乡村旅游到 2019 年年末，小南河村旅游及辣椒酱等农产品营业收入累计达 400 余万元。图为 2020 年 8 月 19 日，驻村第一书记冷菊贞（前左）给游客展示特色服装。（新华社记者王建威摄）

Leng Juzhen (front left), the first Party secretary in Xiaonanhe Village, displays tourists special costumes, Aug. 19, 2020. In 2019, the village in Raohe County, Heilongjiang Province, was selected into the list of the first batch of national key villages to promote tourism. From 2016 to 2019, revenue from tourism and sales of chilli sauce and other produce in the village tops 4 million yuan. (Xinhua/Wang Jianwei)

广袤的云贵高原上，数万名"80后""90后"年轻扶贫干部一头扎进大山深处，成为当地脱贫攻坚的领路人、贫困群众的"主心骨"。图为 2018 年 8 月 28 日拍摄的贵州石阡县五德镇桃子园村第一书记游龙。（新华社发　杨文斌摄）

On the vast Yunnan-Guizhou Plateau, tens of thousands of young poverty alleviation officials born in the 1980s and 1990s have worked hard in deep mountains leading local poverty relief efforts. The photos shows You Long, first Party secretary of Taoziyuan Village of Wude Township, Shiqian County, Guizhou Province, Aug. 28, 2018. (Xinhua/Yang Wenbin)

2017 年 9 月 10 日，西藏驻村工作队队员旦增平措（左）与同事一起生牛粪炉子取暖。（新华社记者赵玉和摄）

Daindzin Puncog (L), a member of a village-based task force in Tibet, warms himself and his colleague with a raw cow dung stove, Sept. 10, 2017. (Xinhua/Zhao Yuhe)

简义相大学毕业辞职回到重庆市黔江区邻鄂镇松林村建起 7 间银耳生产车间，组建了专业种植合作社，随后又成立了农业综合开发公司，带动村民以土地入股的方式种植菊花。如今，入股的 20 户贫困户已全部脱贫。图为 2018 年 9 月 22 日，简义相（左）和父亲打扫自家庭院。（新华社发　杨敏摄）

2018 年 9 月 22 日，简义相在查看金丝皇菊的长势。（新华社发　杨敏摄）

The photo shows Jian checking the growth of yellow chrysanthemums on Sept. 22, 2018. (Xinhua/Yang Min)

After college graduation, Jian resigned and returned to his home village. He built seven tremella planting workshops and a specialized planting cooperative. Later he set up a comprehensive agricultural development company leading villagers to plant chrysanthemums on their land as stakeholders. To date, all the 20 poor households have thrown off poverty in this way. Jian Yixiang (L) cleans up the yard with his father in Songlin Village of Lin'e Township, Qianjiang District, Chongqing Municipality on Sept. 22, 2018. (Xinhua/Yang Min)

2017 年 10 月 23 日拍摄的在毕节市威宁彝族回族苗族自治县石门乡团结村七里冲组脱贫攻坚讲习点，村支书胡钧溥在向当地群众讲解十九大精神及相关的扶贫政策。（新华社记者陶亮摄）

Village Party secretary Hu Junpu explains the spirit of the 19th National Congress of the CPC and poverty relief policies to local people at a workshop in Tuanjie Village of Shimen Township, Weining Yi, Hui and Miao Autonomous County, Bijie City, on Oct. 23, 2017. (Xinhua/Tao Liang)

贵州省铜仁市沿河土家族自治县中寨镇大坪村驻村第一书记文伟红倒在了脱贫攻坚第一线。图为 2018 年 5 月 25 日，文伟红（右三）与村民交流。（新华社发）

Wen, first Party secretary of Daping Village of Zhongzhai Township in Yanhe Tujia Autonomous County, Tongren City, Guizhou Province, died at the front line of poverty relief. The photo shows Wen Weihong (3rd R) talking with villagers on May 25, 2018. (Xinhua)

　　上海姑娘邢翠翠 2009 年来到位于大别山深处的国家级贫困县安徽岳西县黄铺镇鲍岭村，白手起家开始创业，成立畜禽养殖专业合作社，以"公司＋农户"的模式，为周边贫困农户提供兔种、养殖技术、牧草种子和饲料、疫苗等，并负责回收商品兔，让很多贫困村民实现脱贫。图为 2016 年 10 月 11 日，"80 后"邢翠翠在放牛。（新华社记者刘军喜摄）

Xing, a young woman from east China's Shanghai, came to Baoling Village under Huangpu Township of Yuexi, a national level poverty-stricken county deep in Dabie Mountains in 2009. Starting from scratch, she has set up a professional livestock and poultry breeding cooperative that provides poor local farmers with breeding technology, rabbit feed and vaccines, while purchasing rabbits from them. The cooperative has helped many local farmers increase their earnings and shake off poverty. Xing Cuicui herds cattle at Baoling Village of Yuexi County, Anhui Province, Oct. 11, 2016. (Xinhua/Liu Junxi)

宁夏西吉县涵江村第一书记秦振邦（左）在建档立卡贫困户马维仓家了解情况并宣讲扶贫政策。（资料照片　新华社发）

File photo shows Qin Zhenbang (L), first Party secretary of Hanjiang Village of Xiji County in northwest China's Ningxia Hui Autonomous Region, learning about the situation and publicizing the poverty alleviation policy in the family of Ma Weicang, a poor household. (Xinhua/file photo)

2015 年 10 月，清华大学刚毕业工作几个月的硕士潘聪聪，从广西壮族自治区纪委来到百色市田林县潞城瑶族乡丰防村任"第一书记"，帮村里建起了鸡舍，成立了养鸡专业合作社，吸引众多贫困户陆续加入。（新华社记者黄孝邦摄）

Pan Congcong, who just earned a master's degree from Tsinghua University and worked for a few months, came from the Commission for Discipline Inspection of southwest China's Guangxi Zhuang Autonomous Region to Fengfang Village of Lucheng Township in Tianlin County of Baise City to work as the "first Party secretary" in October, 2015. He helped the village build chicken pens and set up specialized cooperatives for raising chickens, attracting many poor households to join one after another. (Xinhua/Huang Xiaobang)

2019 年 8 月 27 日贵州省长顺县广顺镇石洞村第一书记金帼倡（左）给石洞村贫困户陈小林讲解今年的精品水果入股分红政策。（新华社记者齐健摄）

Jin Guochang (L), first Party secretary of Shidong Village of Guangshun Township in Changshun County, southwest China's Guizhou Province, explains to Chen Xiaolin, a poor household in Shidong Village, this year's dividend policy for fine fruits sales on Aug. 27, 2019. (Xinhua/Qi Jian)

广西龙胜各族自治县江柳村是一个以红瑶为主的少数民族村寨，全村 204 户中有 106 户是建档立卡贫困户。2016 年，杨凯从桂林医学院来到江柳村担任驻村第一书记，他带领群众发展农业种植和旅游产业。2018 年，江柳村实现整体脱贫。图为 2020 年 2 月 12 日杨凯（左）和脱贫户潘凤成在规划今年的种植计划。（新华社记者黄孝邦摄）

Yang Kai (L), first Party secretary of Jiangliu Village, Longsheng County of southwest China's Guangxi Zhuang Autonomous Region, plans this year's planting with Pan Fengcheng, a villager lifted out of poverty, Feb. 12, 2020. In Jiangliu, where people from the Red Yao ethnic group take up its majority population, 106 of its 204 households are registered as poor households. In 2016, Yang Kai came to Jiangliu from Guilin Medical College and led the villagers in developing agricultural planting and tourism as the village's first Party secretary. In 2018, Jiangliu shook off poverty overall. (Xinhua/Huang Xiaobang)

　　四川省小金县美兴镇甘家沟村地处大山深处。2017 年年初，安徽来的张飞开始用网络视频宣传甘家沟村及邻近的几个村庄。2019 年 7 月，他和家人在下马厂村云海中就餐时的一条短视频吸引了超千万网友观看，也让这个"云上的村庄"迅速走红。图为甘家沟村的扶贫第一书记张飞（右二）在下马厂村"忘忧云庭"农家餐厅与客人共进午餐。（新华社记者李梦馨摄）

Zhang Fei (2nd R), the first Party secretary of poverty alleviation in Ganjiagou Village of Meixing Township in Xiaojin County of southwest China's Sichuan Province, has lunch with guests at a farm restaurant in Xiamachang Village. Ganjiagou is located deep in the mountains. At the beginning of 2017, Zhang Fei from Anhui began to post online videos to advertise Ganjiagou Village and several neighboring villages. In July 2019, a short video of him and his family eating in the "sea of clouds" in Xiamachang Village attracted more than 10 million netizens to watch, which also made the "village on the cloud" popular quickly. (Xinhua/Li Mengxin)

2019 年 10 月 29 日，安徽省利辛县汝集镇朱集村第一书记、扶贫队队长刘双燕（左）在走访时和村民交谈。2019 年 9 月，刘双燕获 2019 年全国脱贫攻坚奖贡献奖。（新华社发　黄博涵摄）

Liu Shuangyan (L), first Party secretary of Zhuji Village of Ruji Township in Lixin County, east China's Anhui Province, and head of the Poverty Alleviation Team, talks with the villagers during her visit on Oct. 29, 2019. (Xinhua/Huang Bohan)

2020 年 4 月 24 日，广西上林县西燕镇岜独村驻村第一书记康勇（左一）在龟鳖养殖场和养殖能人交流。（新华社记者农冠斌摄）

Kang Yong (1st L), the first Party secretary of Badu Village of Xiyan Township in Shanglin County of southwest China's Guangxi Zhuang Autonomous Region, talks with model breeders at a turtle farm on April 24, 2020. (Xinhua/Nong Guanbin)

2020 年 6 月 3 日河北省邯郸市复兴区委组织部派驻大名县宋尧村驻村第一书记韩献良，通过"贫困户分布图"介绍宋尧村街道硬化情况。韩献良多方联系测绘公司，绘制了一个农户分布图，然后用粉、绿、橙三色彩笔分别把贫困户、低保户、五保户涂上不同颜色，老韩和其他两名驻村队员按图索骥，实现了精准访贫。（新华社发 范世辉摄）

Han Xianliang, first Party secretary of Songyao Village, Daming County, Handan City of north China's Hebei Province, introduces the "Distribution Map of Poor Households" on June 3, 2020. Han Xianliang contacted the surveying and mapping companies in many ways and drew a map of the distribution of farmers. Then he painted different categories of poor households with different colors to realize accurate visits to the poor households. (Xinhua/Fan Shihui)

2020年4月29日，31岁的广西南丹县八圩瑶族乡文家村驻村第一书记黎祖役（左）与村民交流养牛产业发展问题。（新华社记者曹祎铭摄）

Li Zuyi (L), 31, the first Party secretary of Wenjia Village of Baxu Township in Nandan County, southwest China's Guangxi Zhuang Autonomous Region, exchanges views with villagers on the development of cattle industry on April 29, 2020. (Xinhua/Cao Yiming)

2019年9月4日，湖南湘西花垣县十八洞村老支书石顺莲在"十八洞村苗绣特产农民专业合作社"制作苗绣。（新华社发 陈泽国摄）

Shi Shunlian, Party branch secretary of Shibadong Village of Huayuan County, central China's Hunan Province, makes Miao embroidery in farmers' professional cooperatives on Miao embroidery specialty on Sept. 4, 2019. (Xinhua/Chen Zeguo)

2020 年 4 月 12 日，吉林省靖宇县大北山村驻村第一书记高世龙（左）与蛟河市青背村第一书记曾丽圆"直播带货"推介农副产品。（新华社记者许畅摄）

Gao Shilong (L), first Party secretary of Dabeishan Village in Jingyu County, northeast China's Jilin Province, and Zeng Liyuan, first Party secretary of Qingbei Village in Jiaohe City, promote agricultural products online on April 12, 2020. (Xinhua/Xu Chang)

2019 年 3 月 20 日，安徽省金寨县大湾村扶贫队长余静（前左）在指导村民种植茶树。（新华社发　周牧摄）

Yu Jing (Front L), head of the poverty alleviation team in Dawan Village, Jinzhai County, east China's Anhui Province, guides villagers to plant tea trees on March 20, 2019. (Xinhua/Zhou Mu)

法学博士张巍婷，2018 年从国家信访局来到河北省海兴县苏基镇张常丰村任驻村第一书记。她从北京请来专家培训种养殖技术，培养致富带头人、树立特色品牌、推广绿色农产品。图为张巍婷（右）在张常丰村村民代淑凤开办的生产车间了解辣椒酱的销售情况。（新华社记者牟宇摄）

Zhang Weiting, Doctor of Law, came from the National Public Complaints and Proposals Administration to Zhangchangfeng in 2018 as the first Party secretary in the village. She invited experts from Beijing to share breeding techniques, trained models in poverty alleviation, established special brands and promoted green agricultural products. Zhang Weiting (R), first Party secretary of Zhangchangfeng Village, Suji Township, Haixing County of north China's Hebei Province, learns about the sales of chili sauce in the production workshop run by Dai Shufeng, a villager in Zhangchangfeng Village. (Xinhua/Mou Yu)

2019 年 10 月 13 日，黑龙江省绥棱县靠山村党总支第一书记、驻村扶贫工作队队长陈华（左）在与村里的贫困户交谈。（新华社记者王松摄）

Chen Hua (L), first Party secretary of the Party branch of Kaoshan Village in Suiling County, northeast China's Heilongjiang Province, and head of the poverty alleviation team, talks with people from poor households in the village on Oct. 13, 2019. (Xinhua/Wang Song)

　　2019 年 7 月，贵州省锦屏县融媒体中心与该县深度贫困村河口乡加池村结成了帮扶对子。融媒体中心的负责人杨晓琴，吃住在离县城 50 多公里的加池村，与驻村队员一起谋划脱贫之策。图为杨晓琴（左）和队友给群众送农用物资。（新华社记者杨楹摄）

Yang Xiaoqin (L) and her teammates deliver agricultural supplies to villagers. In July 2019, the convergence media center of Jinping County in southwest China's Guizhou Province formed a partnership with Jiachi Village of Hekou Township, a deeply impoverished village in the county. Yang Xiaoqin, head of the center, lived in Jiachi Village which is more than 50 km away from the county seat, and looked for ways to lift the village out of poverty together with village cadres. (Xinhua/Yang Ying)

2019 年 5 月 8 日，湖南溆浦县新桥村残疾贫困户唐付生在山上放羊。双腿残疾的他，几乎每天都要费尽艰辛上山放牛羊，靠骑着一匹马踏出了坚实的脱贫路。（新华社记者白田田摄）

Tang Fusheng, disabled and poor, herds sheep on the mountain in Xinqiao Village of Xupu County in central China's Hunan Province on May 8, 2019. He got out of poverty by herding cattle and sheep on horseback almost every day. (Xinhua/Bai Tiantian)

2019 年 3 月 27 日，在河南省卢氏县沙河乡果角村，"脱贫羊倌"任当锋在喂羊。（新华社记者李嘉南摄）

Ren Dangfeng, a "poverty alleviation shepherd," feeds goats in Guojiao Village, Shahe Town, Lushi County of central China's Henan Province on March 27, 2019. (Xinhua/Li Jianan)

2018 年 5 月 17 日，贵州省沿河土家族自治县中寨镇三会溪村，10 岁时因意外左臂截肢的杨胜强在给放养的山羊补充盐水。2008 年以来，他通过当地市、县残联扶持的安置残疾人就业基金和自筹资金，建起沿河中寨强强养殖农民专业合作社，凭借坚强的毅力将生态山羊养殖做大做强。（新华社发　杨文斌摄）

On May 17, 2018, in Sanhuixi Village, Zhongzhai Township, Yanhe Tujia Autonomous County, southwest China's Guizhou Province, Yang Shengqiang, who had his left arm amputated after an accident when he was 10 years old, feeds saline water to the goats. He set up a cooperative using the funds local governments provided for disabled people and the money he raised himself in 2008, and has since been working hard to develop the ecological goat breeding business. (Xinhua/Yang Wenbin)

扶贫"夫妻档"。左图为 2020 年 6 月 11 日山西省岚县井峪堡村第一书记刘志军在走访村里的养殖户。（新华社记者曹阳摄）右图为 2020 年 6 月 2 日山西省兴县南通村第一书记李翠叶在走访村里的养殖户。（新华社发　刘亮亮摄）

A couple fights for poverty alleviation. The left photo shows Liu Zhijun, first Party secretary to Jingyubao Village of Lanxian County, north China's Shanxi Province, visiting a breeder in the village on June 11, 2020. (Xinhua/Cao Yang) The right photo shows Li Cuiye, first Party secretary to Nantong Village of Xingxian County in Shanxi Province visits a breeder. (Xinhua/Liu Liangliang)

2020 年 1 月 19 日，云南省贡山独龙族怒族自治县独龙江乡巴坡村委会副主任木秋云（右二）召开"火塘会"，邀请长期外出务工返乡的年轻人为扶贫献计献策。（新华社记者赵珮然摄）

Mu Qiuyun (2nd R), deputy director of Bapo Village Committee, Dulongjiang Town, Drung-Nu Autonomous County of Gongshan, southwest China's Yunnan Province, holds a "fireside meeting" on Jan. 19, 2020, inviting young migrant workers to offer poverty alleviation suggestions. (Xinhua/Zhao Peiran)

2019 年 11 月 17 日，青海省玉树藏族自治州玉树市的藏刀匠人更求彭措在制作藏刀刀鞘。（新华社记者张龙摄）

Kunkyap Phuntsog, a Tibetan knife craftsman, makes sheath in Yushu City of Yushu Tibetan Autonomous Prefecture, northwest China's Qinghai Province on Nov. 17, 2019. (Xinhua/Zhang Long)

方荣是湖北省大别山区罗田县希望小学的校长，也是这所小学曾经的学生。童年的经历，让方荣对母校充满感恩。19岁从中等师范毕业后，她义无反顾地选择回母校任教，一待就是十年。图为2019年10月11日，方荣送学生放学回家。（新华社照片 罗田摄）

Fang Rong sends students home on Oct. 11, 2019. She is the headmaster of Hope Primary School of Luotian County in central China's Hubei Province. The school is her alma mater and she is grateful for her experience there. After graduating from secondary normal school at the age of 19, she resolutely chose to teach in her alma mater and stayed there for ten years. (Xinhua/Luo Tian)

2014年，大学毕业在外漂泊6年后，多杰才让听说家乡青海省刚察县建立了扶贫产业示范园，便回乡注册入驻，并在当地政策扶持下购买了第一台牛绒分梳机。订单增多后，县扶贫局帮助他申请各项扶贫发展资金70万元，用于扩大生产规模，为当地贫困牧民解决就业。（新华社记者张宏祥摄）

In 2014, after graduating from university and living far away from home for 6 years, Dorje Tsering heard that his hometown of Gangcha County in northwest China's Qinghai Province had set up a poverty alleviation industrial demonstration park. He returned home to start his own business in the park, and bought the first cow hair sorting machine with the support of local policies. He received 700,000 yuan (about 101,610 U.S. dollars) in various poverty alleviation and development funds with the help of the county's poverty alleviation bureau to expand the scale of production and provided job opportunities for local poor herdsmen. (Xinhua/Zhang Hongxiang)

　　黑龙江省明水县地处大兴安岭南麓集中连片特困地区。崇德镇村民桑庆军少时因家贫辍学外出务工，打拼成为一名工程老板。2019 年 6 月，看好"溜达鸡"市场前景的他返乡承包 30 多亩林地和草原开始饲养"溜达鸡"，他把一条养鸡短视频传到网上，一夜之间他和他的"鸡部队"都成了"网红"。（新华社发　谢剑飞摄）

Mingshui County in northeast China's Heilongjiang Province is located in the southern foot of the Great Khingan Mountains, a poverty-stricken area. Sang Qingjun, born in a poor family in Chongde Township, dropped out of school when he was young and became a project contractor. In June 2019, he went back home and contracted more than 30 mu (2 hectares) of forest land and grassland to raise free range chickens. After posting a short video of him raising the chicken online, he and his "chicken troops" became "internet celebrities." (Xinhua/Xie Jianfei)

四川省派驻凉山的扶贫干部彭杨偶然看到用植物做手工皂的视频，联想到淀粉去污能力很强，就开始拿这里的土豆做试验制作手工皂，结果在网上很受欢迎。（新华社记者吴光于摄）

Peng Yang, a poverty alleviation official stationed in Liangshan Yi Autonomous Prefecture, southwest China's Sichuan Province, once saw a video of making plant-based soap bars and came up with the idea of using potatoes to make soap bars because potatoes are rich in starch and are good in removing dirt. The potato soap bars were very popular online. (Xinhua/Wu Guangyu)

2020 年 3 月 10 日，在四川省美姑县瓦古乡，15 岁的沙马也曲（右）和母亲领到了彭杨制作的土豆手工皂。（新华社记者薛晨摄）

Shama Yechu (R), 15, and her mother receive a handmade potato soap bar made by Peng Yang in Wagu Town, Meigu County, Sichuan Province on March 10, 2020. (Xinhua/Xue Chen)

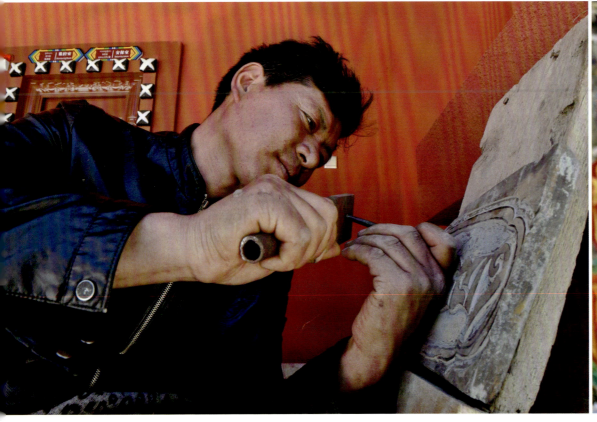

左图为 2020 年 6 月 13 日，四川省壤塘县茸木达乡洞窝村人墨吉在壤塘县棒托石刻公园内制作石刻作品；右图为 2020 年 6 月 13 日，墨吉在展示自己的石刻作品。（新华社记者刘坤摄）

The left photo shows Mo Ji, a native of Dongwo Village, Rongmuda Town, Rangtang County, Sichuan Province, making stone carvings in Bangtuo Stone Carvings Park in Rangtang County on June 13, 2020. The right photo shows Mo Ji displays his stone carvings on June 13, 2020. (Xinhua/Liu Kun)

2013 年，甘肃天祝藏族自治县抓喜秀龙镇南泥沟村宋天柱被认定为建档立卡贫困户后，他经反复思考，决定依靠扶贫贷款发展牛羊养殖。通过几年的奋斗，他已养殖 40 头白牦牛、380 只羊，还成立合作社带动周边村民一起发展规模化养殖。上图为 2020 年 3 月 12 日，宋天柱骑马驱赶羊群。下图为宋天柱和妻子（右）招待亲戚。（新华社记者范培坤摄）

After being identified as poverty-stricken household, Song Tianzhu from Nannigou Village, Tianzhu Tibetan Autonomous County, northwest China's Gansu Province, decided to take poverty alleviation loans to start cattle and sheep farming business. After several years of hard work, he has raised 40 white yaks and 380 sheep, and has set up a cooperative to develop large-scale breeding with his fellow villagers. The upper photo shows Song Tianzhu herding sheep on horseback on March 12, 2020. The lower photo shows Song Tianzhu and his wife (R) entertaining relatives. (Xinhua/Fan Peishen)

　　2019 年 1 月 7 日，在山东省沂源县中庄镇盖冶村草莓扶贫车间，江芳芳（右三）指导村民分拣草莓。江芳芳的草莓产业带动 320 多个农户和 50 个贫困户实现长效增收，她被亲切地称为"草莓姐"。（新华社发　赵东山摄）

On Jan. 7, 2019, Jiang Fangfang (3rd R) teaches villagers how to sort strawberries in the strawberry poverty alleviation workshop in Gaiye Village, Zhongzhuang Town, Yiyuan County, eastern China's Shandong Province. Jiang Fangfang's strawberry business has helped more than 320 farmers and 50 poor households to achieve long-term income increase. She is affectionately called "Strawberry Sister." (Xinhua/Zhao Dongshan)

　　齐敏家住贵州省龙里县洗马镇乐宝村后坝组，幼时患上小儿麻痹症导致行动不便，今年 45 岁的她身高只有 1.3 米。看到乡邻们靠种植辣椒和养猪增收，她也参与其中，通过近十年时间的摸索，终于掌握了一套适合当地的辣椒种植技术。图为 2020 年 5 月 14 日，齐敏和丈夫在搬运辣椒苗。（新华社记者杨文斌摄）

Photo taken on May 14, 2020 shows Qi Min and her husband carrying pepper seedlings. Living in Lebao Village of Longli County in southwest China's Guizhou Province, Qi Min suffered from poliomyelitis in her childhood, leaving her with mobility problems. The 45-year-old is only 1.3 meters tall. Seeing that her neighbors managed to increase their incomes by growing pepper and raising pigs, she also took part in it. After nearly ten years of exploration, she finally mastered a set of pepper planting techniques suitable for the local area. (Xinhua/Yang Wenbin)

贵州省织金县核桃寨青年杨文学用背背篓挣下的钱，带领年轻人，修出了一条越山跨谷、穿寨入户的两公里连寨路。核桃寨的"小康路"也越走越宽。图为杨文学走在连寨路上。（资料照片 新华社发）

File photo shows Yang Wenxue walking on the road he helped build. Yang Wenxue, from Hetao Village in Zhijin County in southwest China's Guizhou Province, led the young men to build a two-kilometer road that crossed mountains and valleys and connected villages and homes with the money he earned from delivering goods using his basket. As people's well-being improves, the village-connecting road is also getting wider. (Xinhua)

安徽省泗县大庄镇曙光村村民孙勇和妻子均为肢体二级残疾，被评定为建档立卡贫困户。在驻村扶贫工作队的帮助下，他们开始了产业脱贫的探索，几经曲折成为鹌鹑养殖户，并利用小额信贷扩大养殖规模，于 2016 年年底成功脱贫。（新华社发 黄博涵摄）

Sun Yong and his wife, both from Shuguang Village in Sixian County of east China's Anhui Province, have secondary physical disabilities and are assessed as an impoverished household. With the help of the poverty alleviation team stationed in the village, they started to work their way out of poverty. After several twists and turns, they became quail farmers and expanded the scale of farming with micro-credit, successfully lifting themselves out of poverty by the end of 2016. (Xinhua/Huang Bohan)

李柳萍出生于广西鹿寨县拉沟乡木龙村。她幼年丧父，家境艰难，曾远赴广东务工，2012 年返乡创办柳鹿山珍特产馆，通过电商平台推介家乡农特产品，并带动贫困户脱贫。图为 2020 年 3 月 10 日拍摄的李柳萍和她的特产馆。（新华社记者黄孝邦摄）

Photo taken on March 10, 2020 shows Li Liuping at her specialty shop. Born in Mulong Village, Luzhai County of south China's Guangxi Zhuang Autonomous Region, Li Liuping lost her father as a child. To support the poor family, Li went to the neighboring Guangdong Province for work. In 2012, she returned home to set up a specialty shop selling agricultural products through e-commerce platforms and helped lift poor households out of poverty. (Xinhua/ Huang Xiaobang)

　　2017 年 10 月，贵州省从江县侗族女孩吴贤艳大学毕业后回到家乡工作，被抽调到加榜乡加车村脱贫攻坚指挥所，当起了一名扶贫网格员。上图为 2020 年 4 月 19 日吴贤艳（左）与村里的大一女生梁琼英在直播推介加榜梯田风光。下图为 2020 年 4 月 18 日吴贤艳（左一）夜访贫困户。（新华社记者杨文斌摄）

In October 2017, Wu Xianyan, a girl of Dong ethnic group from Congjiang County of southwest China's Guizhou Province, returned to her hometown to work after graduating from university. She was transferred to the Jiache Village of Jiabang Township and became a poverty alleviation worker. The upper photo shows Wu Xianyan (L) and Liang Qiongying, a college freshman from the village, introducing the scenery of the terraced fields of Jiabang via live broadcast on April 19, 2020. The lower photo shows Wu Xianyan (L 1st) visiting poor households at night on April 18, 2020. (Xinhua/Yang Wenbin)

在"扶贫日"到来之际，驻守在甘肃少数民族地区的武警某部官兵在驻地广泛开展扶贫帮困活动，为平凉市赵堡村、十里铺村等 5 个行政村的 65 户回、汉族贫困群众修缮房屋、查体看病并赠送米面粮油等生活用品。图为 2015 年 10 月 17 日，武警官兵帮助平凉市宝丰村 75 岁的史秀琴老人采摘玉米。（新华社发　梁兼铭摄）

Armed police officers pick corn for 75-year-old Shi Xiuqin, in Baofeng Village, Pingliang City, northwest China's Gansu Province, Oct. 17, 2015. A squad of armed police stationed in Gansu's ethnic minority areas carries out poverty alleviation activities ahead of the national poverty alleviation day. They repair houses, provide medical check-ups and deliver daily commodities to locals. (Xinhua/Liang Jianming)

2019 年 5 月 19 日，西藏军区某边防部队在放牧点建立党小组帮扶点。（新华社发 张迅摄）

A border defense force in southwest China's Tibet Autonomous Region sets up a Party group support point at a grazing site, May 19, 2019. (Xinhua/Zhang Xun)

2019 年 6 月 20 日，在广西柳州市融水苗族自治县杆洞乡党鸠村木耳种植基地，驻柳空军部队驻党鸠村扶贫工作队队员刘斌（左）查看木耳生长情况。（新华社发 龙杰 摄）

Liu Bin (left), a member of the poverty alleviation task force of the Air Force, checks the growth of fungus at the planting base in Dangjiu Village, Guangxi Zhuang Autonomous Region, June 20, 2019. (Xinhua/Long Jie)

2020 年 6 月 18 日，山东省兰陵县代村党委书记王传喜在查看无土栽培蔬菜长势。2020 年 10 月，王传喜荣获全国脱贫攻坚奖。（新华社记者王阳摄）

Wang Chuanxi, Party secretary of Daicun Village in Lanling County, east China's Shandong Province, checks the growth of vegetables planted in soilless culture, June 18, 2020. He won the national poverty alleviation award in October 2020. (Xinhua/Wang Yang)

2020 年 8 月 4 日，贵州省安顺市平坝区白云镇平元村党支部书记肖正强（左）与贫困户罗振友交流务工情况。2020 年 10 月，肖正强荣获全国脱贫攻坚奖。（新华社记者陶亮摄）

Xiao Zhengqiang (left), Party secretary of Pingyuan Village, Anshun City, Guizhou Province, talks with Luo Zhenyou, a poor resident, Aug. 4, 2020. In October 2020, Xiao won the national poverty alleviation award. (Xinhua/Tao Liang)

2019 年 11 月 14 日，裴春亮（前右）在河南省辉县市张村乡裴寨村与村民（前左）交谈。2020 年 10 月，裴春亮荣获全国脱贫攻坚奖。（新华社记者何娟摄）

Pei Chunliang (front right) talks with a villager (front left) in Peizhai Village, Huixian City, Henan Province, Nov. 14, 2019. In October 2020, Pei won the national poverty alleviation award. (Xinhua/He Juan)

　　韩宇南是河南省周口市国税局进出口税收管理科干部，2015 年被派驻到太康县马厂镇前何行政村担任第一书记。驻村以来，韩宇南扑下身子，沉下心来为村民办实事，向农户推行多元种植模式，种植辣椒、蒜苗、花生等经济作物；在他的影响下，妻子潘丽英也跟他一起驻村。图为 2018 年 1 月 18 日，韩宇南（左四）与村民交流，了解生产生活情况。2020 年 10 月，韩宇南荣获全国脱贫攻坚奖。（新华社记者李安摄）

Han Yunan (fourth from left), learns about production and life of residents in Qianhe Village, central China's Henan Province, Jan. 18, 2018. Han, a taxation official in Zhoukou City, was dispatched to serve as the first Party secretary in Qianhe in 2015. He has promoted the plantation of various cash crops such as chili, garlic sprouts and peanuts to increase income for farmers. His wife also stays in the village with him. In October 2020, Han won the the national poverty alleviation award. (Xinhua/Li An)

2016 年 8 月 4 日，45 岁的刘云军从北京市西城区广外医院来到青海省玉树州人民医院当院长。图为来自北京的援青干部刘云军（左一）带领职工下乡义诊。2020 年 10 月，刘云军荣获全国脱贫攻坚奖。（新华社发　资料照片）

The picture shows Liu Yunjun (first from left), a doctor from Beijing, leads a team to offer free medical checkups for villagers. On Aug. 4, 2016, Liu came to work as president of the People's Hospital in Yushu Tibetan Autonomous Prefecture, northwest China's Qinghai Province. In October 2020, Liu won the the national poverty alleviation award. (Xinhua/file photo)

2017 年 11 月 1 日，在广西上林县塘红乡古春村，黄立温（中）在贫困户潘元芳家了解脱贫情况。黄立温是上林县残联办公室主任，自幼因事故失去双手，被评定为二级双上肢残疾。他主动请缨来到脱贫攻坚一线担任扶贫专干。2020 年 10 月，黄立温荣获全国脱贫攻坚奖。（新华社记者陆波岸摄）

Huang Liwen (middle) talks about poverty alleviation in the house of Pan Yuanfang, a poverty-stricken resident in Guchun Village, Shanglin County, south China's Guangxi Zhuang Autonomous Region, Nov. 1, 2017. Huang, director of the office of Disabled Persons' Federation in Shanglin, lost his hands in an accident during his childhood. He volunteered to serve as a poverty alleviation cadre on the front line. In October 2020, Huang won the national poverty alleviation award. (Xinhua/Lu Boan)

　　支月英是江西省奉新县澡下镇白洋教学点的一名乡村教师。为了让山里孩子也能接受更好的教育，她默默坚守深山 36 载。图为 2016 年 12 月 23 日，支月英在给学生们上语文课。2020 年 10 月，支月英荣获全国脱贫攻坚奖。（新华社记者万象摄）

Zhi Yueying, a rural teacher, gives a Chinese class to students, in Fengxin County, Jiangxi Province, Dec. 23, 2016. She has taught for 36 years. In October 2020, She won the the national poverty alleviation award. (Xinhua/Wan Xiang)

　　经党中央、国务院批准，国务院扶贫开发领导小组在"十三五"期间每年组织开展全国脱贫攻坚奖评选活动，表彰为脱贫攻坚作出突出贡献的组织和个人。组织开展全国脱贫攻坚奖评选表彰，旨在树立脱贫攻坚先进典型，讲好扶贫脱贫故事，展现脱贫攻坚伟大成就，引领社会风尚，弘扬社会主义核心价值观，鼓励全社会进一步行动起来，激励贫困地区广大干部群众进一步行动起来，万众一心，只争朝夕，不负韶华，咬定目标不动摇，一鼓作气、乘势而上，坚决打赢脱贫攻坚战。图为 2020 年 10 月 17 日，2020 年全国脱贫攻坚奖表彰大会现场。

The teleconference at which China honors individuals and institutions with a national award for their outstanding work in poverty alleviation, in Beijing, Oct. 17, 2020. The event aims to promote role models in poverty alleviation, display the great accomplishments of China's poverty-alleviation campaign and encourage the whole society to unite and take further actions to win the battle against poverty.

　　图为 2020 年全国脱贫攻坚奖贡献奖获得者支月英做事迹报告。

Zhi Yueying, winner of the 2020 poverty alleviation award, makes a report on her work at the meeting.

2021 年 2 月 25 日，全国脱贫攻坚总结表彰大会在北京人民大会堂隆重举行。（新华社记者燕雁摄）

A grand gathering is held to mark the nation's poverty alleviation accomplishments and honor model poverty fighters at the Great Hall of the People in Beijing, capital of China, Feb. 25, 2021. (Xinhua/Yan Yan)

2021 年 2 月 25 日，全国脱贫攻坚总结表彰大会在北京人民大会堂隆重举行。图为参会的全国脱贫攻坚楷模荣誉称号获得者在会后合影留念。（新华社记者谢环驰摄）

Role models in China's poverty alleviation fight pose for a group photo after a grand gathering to mark the nation's poverty alleviation accomplishments and honor model poverty fighters at the Great Hall of the People in Beijing, capital of China, Feb. 25, 2021. (Xinhua/Xie Huanchi)

第五部分

PART V

VITALIZATION & VISION

振兴·宏图

我们加强产业扶贫，贫困地区特色优势产业和旅游扶贫、光伏扶贫、电商扶贫等新业态快速发展，增强了贫困地区内生发展活力和动力。通过生态扶贫、易地扶贫搬迁、退耕还林等，贫困地区生态环境明显改善，实现了生态保护和扶贫脱贫一个战场、两场战役的双赢。

　　——2018年2月12日，习近平在打好精准脱贫攻坚战座谈会上的讲话

　　脱贫只是第一步，更好的日子还在后头。

　　——2019年4月10日，习近平给整族脱贫的独龙江乡群众回信

We have strengthened poverty alleviation by developing industries and businesses that leverage local strengths, including new models of poverty alleviation such as tourism, photovoltaic technology and e-commerce programs. This approach has strengthened poor areas' endogenous vitality and motivation for development. By promoting eco-environmental protection, relocating the impoverished population from inhospitable areas to places with better economic prospects, and returning farmland to forest, poor areas have seen significant improvements in the environment and meanwhile good results in poverty alleviation.

—Xi Jinping makes the remarks at the seminar on targeted poverty elimination on Feb. 12, 2018.

Poverty eradication is only the first step, better days are yet to come.

—President Xi Jinping notes in a reply letter to the people in Dulongjiang Township, southwest China's Yunnan Province, April 10, 2019.

2014年1月27日，中共中央总书记、国家主席、中央军委主席习近平在内蒙古锡林郭勒盟81岁的牧民玛吉格家了解生活情况。（新华社记者庞兴雷摄）

President Xi Jinping, also general secretary of the CPC Central Committee and chairman of the CMC, visits an 81-year-old herdsman's family in Xilingol League, north China's Inner Mongolia Autonomous Region, Jan. 27, 2014, asking about their livelihood. (Xinhua/Pang Xinglei)

2013 年 4 月 23 日拍摄的内蒙古锡林郭勒盟乌拉盖管理区哈拉盖图农牧场的草原湖泊。（新华社记者任军川摄）

A grassland lake on a farm in Xilingol League, north China's Inner Mongolia Autonomous Region, April 23, 2013. (Xinhua/Ren Junchuan)

　　2016年7月18日至20日，中共中央总书记、国家主席、中央军委主席习近平在宁夏调研考察。这是7月18日下午，习近平在固原市泾源县大湾乡杨岭村考察时向村民们问好。（新华社记者李涛摄）

President Xi Jinping, also general secretary of the CPC Central Committee and chairman of the CMC, waves to villagers during his visit in Yangling Village, Jingyuan County in northwest China's Ningxia Hui Autonomous Region, July 18, 2016. Xi made an inspection tour in Ningxia from July 18 to 20. (Xinhua/Li Tao)

2020年4月30日无人机拍摄的宁夏泾源县大湾乡杨岭村。(新华社记者冯开华摄)

Yangling Village of Dawan Township in Jingyuan County, northwest China's Ningxia Hui Autonomous Region, April 30, 2020. (Xinhua/Feng Kaihua)

2016 年 11 月 23 日，独龙江畔的云南省贡山独龙族怒族自治县独龙江乡迪政当村的集中安居房一景。
（新华社记者蔺以光摄）

An area of residential houses of Dizhengdang village in Drung-Nu Autonomous County of Gongshan, southwest China's Yunnan Province, Nov. 23, 2016. (Xinhua/Lin Yiguang)

2015年10月7日，寒露将至，福建安溪铁观音秋茶迎来采摘佳期，当地茶农在茶山上忙碌。（新华社发　张九强摄）

Farmers pick tea leaves in Anxi County, east China's Fujian Province, Oct. 7, 2015. (Xinhua/Zhang Jiuqiang)

2014 年 9 月 13 日，糯扎渡大坝。（新华社发）

The Nuozhadu dam, southwest China's Yunnan Province, Sept. 13, 2014. (Xinhua)

2014 年 9 月 15 日，糯扎渡水电站。糯扎渡水电站横拦澜沧江，位于云南普洱市境内，因攻破世界级水利难关而收获了多项第一。与此同时，科研人员积极探索研究保护环境和生物多样性的措施，在取得水电开发与生态保护双赢路上留下了独特的生态印迹。（新华社发）

The Nuozhadu hydropower station on the Lancang River in Pu'er City, Yunnan Province, wins many firsts for overcoming world-class technical difficulties in water conservancy projects. Researchers actively explore measures to protect the environment and biodiversity and achieve a win-win outcome on hydropower development and ecological protection, Sept, 15, 2014. (Xinhua)

2016 年 1 月 18 日航拍的刚建成通车的恩黔高速（湖北恩施至重庆黔江）朝阳寺特大桥。（新华社发　宋文摄）

An elevated bridge of Enshi-Qianjiang expressway linking central China's Hubei Province and its neighbor Chongqing Municipality, Jan. 18, 2016. (Xinhua/ Song Wen)

2016 年 6 月 27 日，青藏铁路列车经过拉萨。（新华社记者普布扎西摄）

A train passes through Lhasa, capital of southwest China's Tibet Autonomous Region, on the Qinghai-Tibet Railway, the world's highest rail system, June 27, 2016. (Xinhua/Phurbu Tashi)

2017 年 2 月 9 日，太阳露出地平线，转场的羊群在西藏浪卡子县普莫雍错冰面投下纤长的蓝色影子。（新华社记者普布扎西摄）

The sun rises above the horizon as herds of sheep cast slender blue shadows on the icy surface of Puma Yumco Lake in southwest China's Tibet Autonomous Region, Feb. 9, 2017. (Xinhua/Phurbu Tashi)

2017 年 9 月 22 日无人机拍摄的吉林省和龙市光东村秋日稻田。（新华社发　许畅摄）

Paddy fields in Guangdong Village, Helong City, northeast China's Jilin Province, Sept. 22, 2017. (Xinhua/Xu Chang)

2016年5月27日拍摄的吉林省和龙市光东村水稻种植户在进行机械插秧。（新华社发 林宏摄）

Farmers transplant rice seedlings in Guangdong Village, Helong City, northeast China's Jilin Province, May 27, 2016. (Xinhua/Lin Hong)

2019 年 4 月 9 日清晨无人机拍摄的云海笼罩的西藏墨脱县。（新华社记者李鑫摄）

Metok County, southwest China's Tibet Autonomous Region, is shrouded in clouds in the grey light of the dawn, April 9, 2019. (Xinhua/Li Xin)

2017 年 3 月 30 日，鸟瞰西藏墨脱公路。墨脱公路 2013 年 10 月 31 日正式通车，标志着我国实现了"县县通公路"的目标。（新华社记者普布扎西摄）

A bird's eye view of Metok Highway in Tibet Autonomous Region on March 30, 2017. The Metok Highway opens to traffic on Oct. 31, 2013, which means highways have connected all counties across the country. (Xinhua/Phurbu Tashi)

2018 年 3 月 9 日无人机拍摄的贵州省六盘水市六枝特区木岗镇的油菜花田。（新华社记者陶亮摄）

Rape flower fields in Mugang Township of Liupanshui City, southwest China's Guizhou Province, March 9, 2018. (Xinhua/Tao Liang)

依托四好农村路建设发展生态茶叶、有机稻谷和精品水果产业，贵州湄潭县金花村实现农民人均年增收 8000 多元。图为 2018 年 4 月 12 日，车辆行驶在金花村内的道路上。（新华社记者刘续摄）

Vehicles run on the road in Jinhua Village, Meitan County, southwest China's Guizhou Province, April 12, 2018. Thanks to the construction of better roads, Meitan County has better conditions in developing industries such as growing ecological tea, organic rice and fruits, increasing the per capita annual income of farmers by more than 8,000 yuan. (Xinhua/Liu Xu)

2018 年 4 月 10 日无人机拍摄的晨曦中的湖北省蕲春县雾云山梯田。雾云山村利用高山梯田风光，打造农耕文化景区，观光农业成为当地农民脱贫致富的新途径。（新华社记者程敏摄）

Terraced lands on Wuyun Mountain in Qichun County of central China's Hubei Province, April 10, 2018. Local farmers take advantage of the scenery of high mountain terraces to develop tourism. Sightseeing agriculture becomes a new route to poverty alleviation. (Xinhua/Cheng Min)

2018 年 7 月 17 日无人机拍摄的宁夏固原市隆德县观庄乡前庄村的农田与苍翠的六盘山。（新华社记者王鹏摄）

The lush Liupan mountain and the farmland in Qianzhuang Village, Longde County, northwest China's Ningxia Hui Autonomous Region, July 17, 2018. (Xinhua/Wang Peng)

2018 年 8 月 4 日无人机拍摄的一辆汽车行驶在陕西省榆林市横山区沙漠治理与未治理的分界公路上。（新华社记者陶明摄）

A car rides on a road in Hengshan District, Yulin City, northwest China's Shaanxi Province. The road is also the boundary of regions with or without desert control, Aug. 4, 2018. (Xinhua/Tao Ming)

2018 年 9 月 22 日无人机拍摄的贵州省金沙县的乌江。（新华社记者欧东衢摄）

Wujiang River in Jinsha County, southwest China's Guizhou Province, Sept. 22, 2018. (Xinhua/Ou Dongqu)

改革开放 40 多年，中国绿色版图不断扩大——从 12% 到 2020 年的 22.96%，森林覆盖率几乎翻了一番。上图为治理前，山西省右玉县的荒凉沙地（资料照片）。下图为 2018 年 8 月 7 日拍摄的右玉县小南山森林公园（新华社记者曹阳摄）。

Since the reform and opening-up, China's forest coverage has been steadily increasing, rising from 12 percent to 22.96 precent in 2020. The picture at the top shows the bleak sandy lands in Youyu County, Shanxi Province before environmental protection efforts. (file photo) The picture at the bottom, which was taken on August 7, 2018, shows a forest park in Youyu. (Xinhua/Cao Yang)

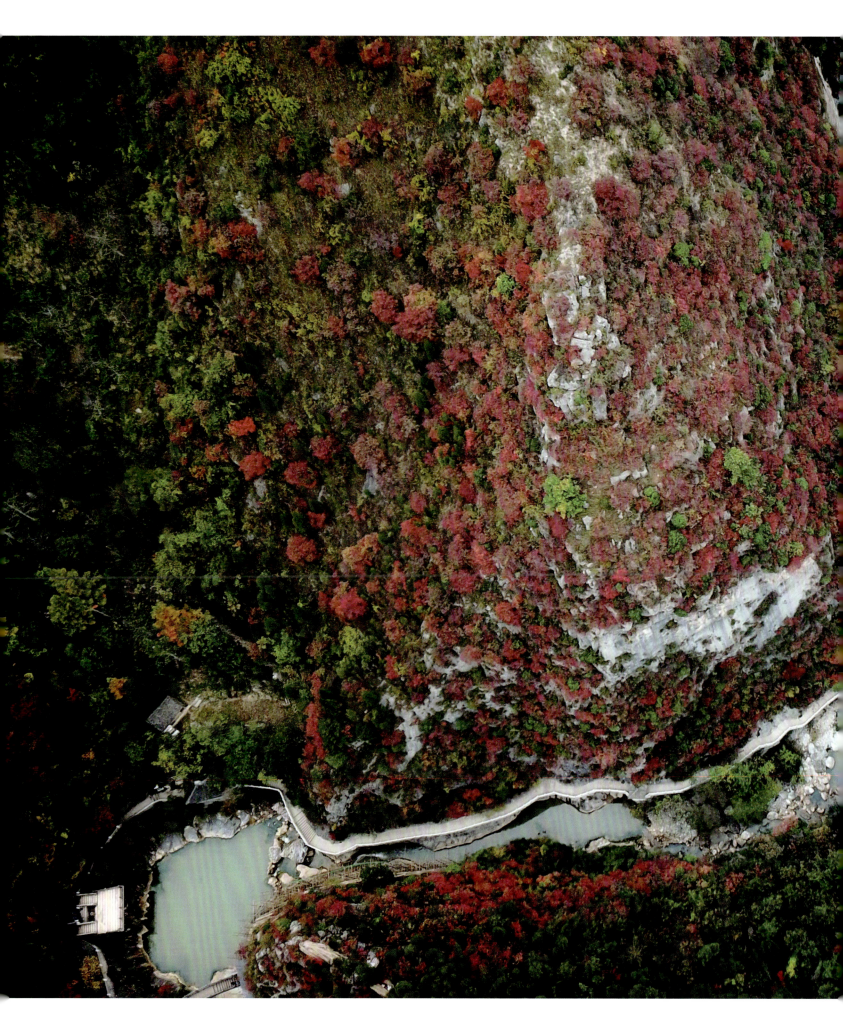

2018 年 10 月 16 日无人机拍摄的甘肃成县西狭颂景区层林尽染，峡内石崖、池潭、树木、山峰构成五彩斑斓的秋日美景图，引人入胜。（新华社记者陈斌摄）

The splendid autumn scenery of Xixiasong in Chengxian County, northwest China's Gansu Province, Oct. 16, 2018. (Xinhua/Chen Bin)

2018 年 9 月 4 日无人机拍摄的绿意盎然的宁夏贺兰山。（新华社记者王鹏摄）

The lush Helan Mountains in Ningxia Hui Autonomous Region, Sept. 4, 2018. (Xinhua/Wang Peng)

2018 年 9 月 17 日无人机拍摄的西藏阿里地区日土县日松乡甲岗村的苗圃基地。（新华社记者旦增尼玛曲珠摄）

A nursery garden in Jiagang Village, Risum Township, Tibet's Ali Prefecture, Sept. 17, 2018. (Xinhua/Tenzin Nyima Chodru)

2019 年 9 月 16 日，在云南省迪庆藏族自治州普达措国家公园内，牲畜在洛茸村民小组附近的草甸上吃草。（新华社记者张誉东摄）

Livestock graze on a meadow in the Potatso National Park in the Deqen Tibetan Autonomous Prefecture, southwest China's Yunnan Province, Sept. 16, 2019. (Xinhua/Zhang Yudong)

2019 年 1 月 11 日拍摄的通往西藏拉萨市的高等级公路。（新华社记者普布扎西摄）

A high-grade highway leading to Lhasa, capital of southwest China's Tibet Autonomous Region, Jan. 11, 2019.
(Xinhua/Phurbu Tashi)

2019 年 8 月 13 日无人机拍摄的宁夏彭阳县旱作梯田。（新华社记者冯开华摄）

Dry terraces in Pengyang County, northwest China's Ningxia Hui Autonomous Region, Aug. 13, 2019. (Xinhua/Feng Kaihua)

2019 年 4 月 25 日无人机拍摄的重庆市黔江区太极乡李子村的立体农业基地 。（新华社发　杨敏摄）

Three-dimensional agricultural base in Lizi Village, Taiji Township, southwest China's Chongqing Municipality, April 25, 2019. (Xinhua/Yang Min)

2019 年 9 月 13 日无人机拍摄的西藏拉萨市尼木玛曲河和两岸错落有致的农田。（新华社记者晋美多吉摄）

Cropland dotting Nyemo Marchu River in Lhasa, capital of southwest China's Tibet Autonomous Region, Sept. 13, 2019. (Xinhua/Jigme Dorje)

图为 2019 年 9 月 4 日无人机拍摄的河南省光山县文殊乡东岳村附近的稻田。（新华社记者冯大鹏摄）

Rice fields near Dongyue Village, Guangshan County, central China's Henan Province, Sept. 4, 2019. (Xinhua/Feng Dapeng)

2019 年 6 月 2 日无人机拍摄的重庆市黔江区小南海镇桥梁村古枫寨一角。（新华社发　杨敏摄）

An traditional ethnic village in Xiaonanhai Township, southwest China's Chongqing Municipality, June 2, 2019. (Xinhua/Yang Min)

决战决胜 中国脱贫攻坚的伟大实践　SECURING A FINAL VICTORY China's Poverty Reduction Practice

2019 年 6 月 20 日拍摄的贵州省威宁彝族回族苗族自治县草海国家级自然保护区一隅。（新华社记者陶亮摄）

Scenery at the Caohai National Nature Reserve in Weining Yi, Hui and Miao Autonomous County, southwest China's Guizhou Province, June 20, 2019. (Xinhua/Tao Liang)

2019 年 3 月 23 日，贵州省思剑高速公路剑河县岑松镇段。（新华社记者杨文斌摄）

A section of the Sinan-Jianhe expressway in southwest China's Guizhou Province, March 23, 2019. (Xinhua/Yang Wenbin)

2019 年 12 月 27 日无人机拍摄的广西融水苗族自治县杆洞乡党鸠村乌英苗寨，村民在吃百家宴。（新华社记者黄孝邦摄）

Villagers enjoy a feast in Dangjiu Village of Rongshui Miao Autonomous County, south China's Guangxi Zhuang Autonomous Region on Dec. 27, 2019. (Xinhua/Huang Xiaobang)

　　陕西省安康市汉滨区曾经是贫困人口超过 10 万人的深度贫困县区，这里的多数贫困群众居住在秦巴山区的大山深处。近年来，汉滨区帮助不适宜易地移民搬迁的部分危房户进行危房改造，同时与农村人居环境改善相结合，建设配套生活设施，美化房屋周边环境，使群众安居乐业。图为 2018 年 10 月 29 日拍摄的汉滨区茨沟镇西沟村村民方献林（右）家里经过改造翻新的房屋和院子。（新华社记者邵瑞摄）

A renovated house and courtyard in Xigou Village, Hanbin District, Oct. 29, 2018. Hanbin District of Ankang City, northwest China's Shaanxi Province, was an impoverished area with a poor population of more than 100,000. Most of the poor people here live in remote mountainous areas. In recent years, the local government helps residents living in areas not suitable for relocation to renovate their dilapidated homes, build supporting living facilities and improve the surrounding environment to enable them to live and work comfortably. (Xinhua/Shao Rui)

　　20 万亩万寿菊盛开南疆助脱贫。图为 2020 年 6 月 16 日，在新疆莎车县英吾斯塘乡，25 岁的吾热古丽·吾斯曼将采摘好的万寿菊装到电动三轮车上。（新华社记者李志浩摄）

About 13,300 hectares of marigold flowers bloom in the southern part of northwest China's Xinjiang Uygur Autonomous Region to help people shake off poverty. Huregul Husman, 25, loads marigold flowers onto an electric tricycle in Yengiostang Township of Yarkant County in Xinjiang on June 16, 2020. (Xinhua/Li Zhihao)

　　2019 年 9 月 6 日，新疆和田县一家农民专业合作社，农民在分拣核桃。（新华社记者丁磊摄）

Farmers sort walnuts at a rural cooperative in Hotan County, northwest China's Xinjiang Uygur Autonomous Region on Sept. 6, 2019. (Xinhua/Ding Lei)

2019 年 6 月 5 日无人机拍摄的西藏拉鲁湿地。（新华社记者普布扎西摄）

An aerial view taken with a drone shows the Lhalu wetland in southwest China's Tibet Autonomous Region, June 5, 2019. (Xinhua/Phurbu Tashi)

河北省武安市将花椒产业作为脱贫增收的重要抓手，因地制宜扩大种植规模，全市花椒种植面积达 12 万亩。图为 2020 年 8 月 9 日，武安市徘徊镇后李甲村农民在晾晒采摘的花椒。（新华社记者王晓摄）

Wu'an City in north China's Hebei Province develops the Sichuan pepper industry as an important approach to shaking off poverty and increasing income, expands planting in according to local conditions and has a total planting area of 8,000 hectares. Farmers dry the Sichuan pepper in Houlijia Village in Wu'an on Aug. 9, 2020. (Xinhua/Wang Xiao)

　　2020 年 8 月 11 日，在黑龙江省宁安市庆雨蔬菜专业合作社蔬菜产业园基地，工人把刚采摘下来的西红柿打包装箱。（新华社记者王建威摄）

Workers pack fresh tomatoes at a vegetable industrial base in Ning'an City, northeast China's Heilongjiang Province, Aug. 11, 2020. (Xinhua/Wang Jianwei)

图为 2019 年 10 月 13 日，新疆博湖县塔温觉肯乡辣椒晾晒场。（新华社记者丁磊摄）

Peppers are dried on a field in Bagrax County, northwest China's Xinjiang Uygur Autonomous Region on Oct. 13, 2019. (Xinhua/Ding Lei)

2019 年 10 月 23 日无人机拍摄的位于西藏八宿县境内的"怒江 72 拐"，这是川藏线上一段艰险与美景并存的山路。（新华社记者江宏景摄）

A winding mountain road with breathtaking views on the Sichuan-Tibet Highway in Baxoi County, southwest China's Tibet Autonomous Region, Oct. 23, 2019. (Xinhua/Jiang Hongjing)

2019 年 10 月 23 日，318 国道西藏八宿县 72 拐边的同尼村。（新华社记者江宏景摄）

Tangnyi Village in Baxoi County in southwest China's Tibet Autonomous Region, Oct. 23, 2019. (Xinhua/Jiang Hongjing)

2019 年 12 月 18 日无人机拍摄的黑龙江省抚远市海青乡海兴村一角。（新华社发　谢剑飞摄）

Haixing Village in Fuyuan City, northeast China's Heilongjiang Province, Dec. 18, 2019. (Xinhua/Xie Jianfei)

2019 年 10 月 23 日，西藏浪卡子县普玛江塘乡那木其村的新房。江塘乡是中国海拔最高乡。（新华社发）

New houses in Namqi Village of Pumachangtang Township, the highest township in China, in Nagarze County, southwest China's Tibet Autonomous Region, Oct. 23, 2019. (Xinhua)

2019 年 7 月 22 日拍摄的四川省布拖县乐安乡洛恩村新貌。（新华社记者江宏景摄）

The new look of Luo'en Village in Butuo County, southwest China's Sichuan Province, July 22, 2019. (Xinhua/Jiang Hongjing)

图为 2020 年 8 月 12 日拍摄的甘肃省甘南藏族自治州卓尼县阿子滩镇阿子滩村。（新华社记者邢广利摄）

A picture of Azitan Village, Gannan Tibetan Autonomous Prefecture, northwest China's Gansu Province, Aug. 12, 2020. (Xinhua/Xing Guangli)

2018 年 1 月 9 日，重庆市新白沙沱长江特大桥（右）和修建于 20 世纪 50 年代的白沙沱长江大桥（左）。（新华社记者刘潺摄）

The new Baishatuo Bridge (R) and an old one built in 1950s (L) on the Yangtze River in southwest China's Chongqing Municipality, Jan. 9, 2018. (Xinhua/Liu Chan)

　　2019年12月30日，云雾缭绕中的贵州平塘特大桥。该桥横跨峡谷，连接罗甸、平塘两县，全长2135米，通车后成为连接贵州南部的交通要道。（新华社记者刘续摄）

The Pingtang bridge in southwest China's Guizhou Province, Dec. 30, 2019. With a total length of 2,135 meters, it spans over a deep canyon to connect the counties of Luodian and Pingtang, becoming a major traffic route in southern Guizhou. (Xinhua/Liu Xu)

　　2017年4月4日，一场春雨过后，位于湖北省恩施土家族苗族自治州境内的沪渝高速泗渡河大桥周围云雾缭绕，宛如仙境。（新华社发　文林摄）

A bridge in Enshi Tujia and Miao Autonomous Prefecture, central China's Hubei Province, is enveloped by cloud and mist after a spring rain on April 4, 2017. (Photo by Wen Lin/Xinhua)

杭瑞高速贵州省毕节至都格（黔滇界）公路北盘江大桥上云雾缭绕，北盘江大桥主桥跨径 720 米，桥面到谷底垂直高度 565 米，相当于 200 层楼高，为目前世界第一高桥。图为 2018 年 8 月 9 日无人机航拍的北盘江大桥。（新华社记者欧东衢摄）

The Beipanjiang River Bridge in southwest China's Guizhou Province, Aug. 9, 2018. It is the highest bridge in the world, with a span of 720 meters on the main structure and a vertical height of 565 meters from the bridge deck to the valley bottom, which is equivalent to the height of a 200-story building. (Xinhua/Ou Dongqu)

图为 2019 年 8 月 8 日无人机拍摄的福建省寿宁县下党乡下党村。（新华社记者林善传传摄）

Xiadang Village in Shouning County, east China's Fujian Province, Aug. 8, 2019. (Xinhua/Lin Shanchuan)

2019 年 11 月 21 日无人机拍摄的阿尔山城市景观。阿尔山市位于内蒙古兴安盟西北部，横跨大兴安岭西南山麓。近年来，当地实施一系列城市景观改造项目，边陲小城美景尽显。（新华社记者彭源摄）

The urban landscape of Aershan City, Nov. 21, 2019. Aershan is located in the northwestern part of Xing'an League in north China's Inner Mongolia Autonomous Region, spanning the southwestern foothills of the Great Khingan Range. In recent years, a series of urban renovation projects have made the border town more beautiful. (Xinhua/Peng Yuan)

　　吉林省辉南县是"吉林大米"主产区之一。在辉南县兴德村，活跃着几位青年创业者，他们采用"公司＋合作社＋农户"合作形式，专注水稻有机种植，帮助当地农民致富增收。图为 2019 年 5 月 30 日无人机拍摄的陆晓泉（右）与王超平在田埂上查看水稻插秧情况。（新华社记者张楠摄）

Huinan County is a major rice production area in northeast China's Jilin Province. In Xingde Village, young entrepreneurs focus on organic rice cultivation to help local farmers to increase their income through cooperation among enterprises, cooperatives and farmers. Lu Xiaoquan (R) and Wang Chaoping check rice seedling planting on May 30, 2019. (Xinhua/Zhang Nan)

西江千户苗寨、郎德苗寨位于贵州省黔东南苗族侗族自治州雷山县，距离沪昆高铁凯里南站均不到50公里的路程。近年来，当地不断推动高铁资源和旅游景区深度融合，方便各地游客前来体验苗族风情，观赏苗寨美景，为古老苗寨的乡村振兴注入活力。图为2016年6月22日，一列动车组列车行驶在凯里境内。（新华社发　吴吉斌摄）

A train runs in Kaili City, southwest China's Guizhou Province, June 22, 2016. Xijiangqianhu and Langde are two Miao ethnic villages in Leishan County, Guizhou. The two villages are less than 50 km away from Kaili high-speed railway station. In recent years, the local government has made use of the railway to develop tourism. (Xinhua/Wu Jibin)

2020 年 6 月 30 日无人机拍摄的一辆四川乡村客运面包车行驶在布拖县阿布洛哈村新完工的村道上。（新华社记者江宏景摄）

A passenger van runs on a newly completed road in Abuluoha Village of Butuo County, southwest China's Sichuan Province on June 30, 2020. (Xinhua/Jiang Hongjing)

2019 年 3 月 26 日拍摄的福建省武夷山市星村镇的生态茶山。（新华社记者魏培全摄）

An ecological tea-growing mountain in Xingcun Township of Wuyishan City, east China's Fujian Province, March 26, 2019. (Xinhua/Wei Peiquan)

2019 年 6 月 13 日无人机拍摄的江西省于都县段屋乡寒信村。（新华社记者周密摄）

Hanxin Village of Duanwu Township in Yudu County, east China's Jiangxi Province, June 13, 2019. (Xinhua/Zhou Mi)

1988年，我国建立了以"开发扶贫、生态建设"为主题的毕节试验区，通过采取一切有利于脱贫的措施，当地 30 年累计减贫 594 万人，森林覆盖率大幅提高。其扶贫实践为我国反贫困斗争积累了宝贵经验。图为 2018 年 7 月 23 日，贵州省毕节市赫章县河镇乡海雀村新貌。（新华社记者杨文斌摄）

Photo taken on July 23, 2018 shows the new look of Haique Village in Bijie City, southwest China's Guizhou Province. In 1988, China established a pilot area in Bijie focusing on "poverty alleviation through development and ecological construction". By taking a series of measures, 5.94 million people shook off poverty in 30 years and the forest coverage rate greatly increased. Bijie's practice has provided valuable experience for China's fight against poverty. (Xinhua/Yang Wenbin)

2016 年 3 月 27 日，一对野生大熊猫在陕西省佛坪县岳坝镇大古坪村活动。（新华社记者陶明摄）

Two wild giant pandas wander in Daguping Village of Foping County, northwest China's Shaanxi Province on March 27, 2016. (Xinhua/Tao Ming)

2019 年 2 月 21 日在贵州省威宁县草海国家级自然保护区内拍摄的黑颈鹤。（新华社发 胡攀学摄）

Black-necked cranes at the Caohai National Nature Reserve in Weining Yi, Hui and Miao Autonomous County, southwest China's Guizhou Province, Feb. 21, 2019. (Photo by Hu Panxue/Xinhua)

　　2017 年，陕西省扶贫办宣布：佛坪县脱贫摘帽，退出贫困县序列。这对于生态保护具有极大的促进作用。图为 2018 年 8 月 3 日拍摄的陕西省佛坪县熊猫谷内拍摄的秦岭金丝猴。（新华社记者刘潇摄）

The golden snub-nosed monkeys were seen in the Qinling Mountains, in Foping County of northwest China's Shaanxi Province, Aug. 3, 2018. The provincial poverty alleviation and development office announced in 2017 that Foping shook off poverty and was removed from a list of the poverty-stricken counties, which is greatly conducive to ecological protection. (Xinhua/Liu Xiao)

　　洋县雷草沟水库附近拍摄的朱鹮（2020 年 8 月 2 日摄）。在洋县，随处可见成群结队的朱鹮在汉江及汉江支流的河滩和湿地觅食、栖息。朱鹮是陕西省汉中市洋县的一张靓丽名片，正成为脱贫群众奔小康的一把"金钥匙"。（新华社记者兰红光摄）

Crested ibis near Leicaogou Reservoir in Yangxian County, Shaanxi Province, Aug. 2, 2020. In Yangxian, groups of crested ibis can be seen everywhere in the river beaches and wetlands of the Hanjiang River and its tributaries, feeding and resting. (Xinhua/Lan Hongguang)

2019 年 4 月 18 日，云雾缭绕的云南独龙江峡谷，高黎贡山与担当力卡山夹江而立。（新华社记者江文耀摄）

The Dulongjiang River valley with Gaoligong Mountain and Dandanglika Mountain erecting on both sides, April 18, 2019. (Xinhua/ Jiang Wenyao)

2020 年 5 月 15 日无人机拍摄的湖南省永顺县芙蓉镇。（新华社发　陈思汗摄）

Furong Township of Yongshun County in central China's Hunan Province, May 15, 2020. (Photo by Chen Sihan/Xinhua)

2018 年 1 月 20 日，苗族群众在贵州省丹寨县排调镇甲石村管护茶场。（新华社记者杨文斌摄）

People of the Miao ethnic group work in a tea farm in Danzhai County of southwest China's Guizhou Province, Jan. 20, 2018. (Xinhua/Yang Wenbin)

2017 年 9 月 23 日无人机拍摄的贵州省锦屏县固本乡东庄村苗寨梯田金秋景象。（新华社记者杨文斌摄）

The autumn scenery at terraced fields in Dongzhuang Village, which is inhabited by people of the Miao ethnic group, in Guben Township of Jinping County, southwest China's Guizhou Province, Sept. 23, 2017. (Xinhua/Yang Wenbin)

2019 年 4 月 7 日无人机拍摄的广西龙胜各族自治县和平乡的平安村。（新华社记者曹祎铭摄）

Ping'an Village of Heping Township in Longsheng County, south China's Guangxi Zhuang Autonomous Region, April 7, 2019. (Xinhua/Cao Yiming)

第六部分

PART VI

丰收·喜庆

HARVEST & CELEBRATION

脱贫攻坚时间紧、任务重，必须真抓实干、埋头苦干。各级党委和政府要以更加昂扬的精神状态、更加扎实的工作作风，团结带领广大干部群众坚定信心、顽强奋斗，万众一心夺取脱贫攻坚战全面胜利。

——2018 年 6 月，习近平对脱贫攻坚工作作出重要指示强调

脱贫摘帽不是终点，而是新生活、新奋斗的起点。接下来要做好乡村振兴这篇大文章，推动乡村产业、人才、文化、生态、组织等全面振兴。

——2020 年 4 月 20 日至 23 日，习近平在陕西考察时指出

The task of eliminating poverty is arduous and the time is pressing. It requires solid and hard efforts. With higher morale and a more down-to-earth work style, Party committees and governments at all levels should unite and lead the cadres and the people to strengthen their confidence and work tenaciously to secure an all-round victory in the battle against poverty.

—Xi Jinping makes the remarks on poverty alleviation in June 2018.

Being lifted out of poverty is not an end in itself but the starting point of a new life and a new pursuit. Next, progress must be secured in rural vitalization so that all-round vitalization can be achieved in rural industries, talent, culture, ecological environment and organization work.

—Xi Jinping makes the remarks during an inspection tour in Shaanxi Province from April 20 to 23, 2020.

2016 年 8 月 22 日至 24 日，中共中央总书记、国家主席、中央军委主席习近平在青海调研考察。图为 8 月 22 日下午，习近平在海西蒙古族藏族自治州格尔木市唐古拉山镇长江源村藏族村民申格家中同一家人亲切交谈。（新华社记者兰红光摄）

President Xi Jinping, also general secretary of the CPC Central Committee and chairman of the CMC, talks with the family of Sengye, a Tibetan in Changjiangyuan Village, Golmud City in northwest China's Qinghai Province, Aug. 22, 2016. Xi made an inspection tour in Qinghai from Aug. 22 to 24, 2016. (Xinhua/Lan Hongguang)

2018 年 9 月 30 日，在青海省格尔木市唐古拉镇长江源村，几名学生走在放学回家的路上。（新华社记者田文杰摄）

A few students walk their way home after school in Changjiangyuan Village, Tanggula Township in Qinghai Province, Sept. 30, 2018. (Xinhua/Tian Wenjie)

2014 年 7 月 2 日，在广西龙胜各族自治县龙脊镇金坑瑶寨，一名女子站在晒满红瑶衣服的木楼上。每年农历六月初六，当地都要欢庆传统节日"晒衣节"。（新华社记者陆波岸摄）

A woman stands inside a wooden rural dwelling where clothes of the Yao ethnic group are hung up in Jinkeng Yao Village, Longji Township, Guangxi Zhuang Autonomous Region, July 2, 2014. Local people celebrate the "Clothes Drying Day," a traditional festival, on the sixth day of the sixth lunar month each year. (Xinhua/Lu Boan)

2015 年 7 月 14 日，广西东兰县三弄瑶族乡瑶族同胞摆起瑶寨长宴，庆祝一年一度的传统节日"祝箸节"。（新华社发　高东风摄）

The Yao people attend a long-table dinner in Sannong township, Donglan County, Guangxi Zhuang Autonomous Region, to celebrate the annual traditional Zhuzhu Festival, July 14, 2015. (Photo by Gao Dongfeng/Xinhua)

2016 年 12 月 29 日，渔民杨再平在贵州省剑河县仰阿莎湖上捕鱼，准备供应节日市场。（新华社记者杨文斌摄）

Yang Zaiping, a fisherman in Jianhe County, Guizhou Province, catches fish on Yang'asha Lake for sale during the holiday season, Dec. 29, 2016. (Xinhua/Yang Wenbin)

陕西洛南县对全县愿意到敬老院的 381 名农村特困人员实行集中供养政策。图为 2020 年 7 月 28 日洛南县灵口区域敬老院的老人们在唱静板书。（新华社记者刘潇摄）

Luonan County of Shaanxi Province provides centralized old-age care for 381 elderly farmers from poverty-stricken households who are willing to participate in the project. Elderly people in a nursing home play musical instruments, July 28, 2020. (Xinhua/Liu Xiao)

2016 年 12 月 1 日，福建省建瓯市徐墩镇丰乐新村 51 岁的贫困户杨廷钦（右）和 73 岁的母亲魏瑞姬在扶贫搬迁的新居门前合影。（新华社记者张国俊摄）

Yang Tingqin (R) and his 73-year-old mother Wei Ruiji take a photo in front of their new home thanks to a relocation project to help poverty-stricken households like themselves in Fengle Village, Jian'ou City, Fujian Province, Dec 1, 2016. (Xinhua/Zhang Guojun)

2017 年以来，甘肃省积石山县加大推进免费学前教育和农村幼儿园精准建设项目，通过优化农村学前教育资源配置来调整农村幼儿园布局，实现了 1500 人以上的行政村免费幼儿园全覆盖。图为 2017 年 3 月 29 日，积石山县刘集乡刘集幼儿园的小朋友在游乐室玩耍。（新华社记者陈斌摄）

Since 2017, Jishishan County in Gansu Province has pushed ahead with free preschool education and the construction of kindergartens in rural areas. The county has ensured kindergarten education at all administrative villages with a population of 1,500 people or above. Children play in a kindergarten, March 29, 2017. (Xinhua/Chen Bin)

2020 年 6 月 14 日，在四川省阿坝县民族寄宿制小学内的少年宫里，孩子们学习用传统乐器曼陀铃进行弹唱。（新华社记者刘坤摄）

Students learn to play Mandolin, a traditional musical instrument, at the Children's Palace in a boarding primary school in Sichuan Province's Aba County, June 14, 2020. (Xinhua/Liu Kun)

2017 年 6 月 16 日，陕西省安康市汉滨区双龙镇杜坝村的五四小学附设幼儿园，小朋友们在操场上做游戏。（新华社记者邵瑞摄）

Children play games at a kindergarten afflicted with a primary school in Duba Village, Ankang City, Shaanxi Province, June 16, 2017. (Xinhua/Shao Rui)

2016 年 9 月 1 日，在四川省喜德县拉克乡四合村幼儿教学点内，老师在给小朋友们讲故事。（新华社记者刘坤摄）

A teacher tells children stories at Sihe Village, Xide County, Sichuan Province, Sept. 1, 2016. (Xinhua/Liu Kun)

2016 年 11 月 25 日，云南省福贡县匹河怒族乡托坪村委会托坪小组的怒族男孩李雪聪（左）和麻富贵向山下眺望。（新华社记者胡超摄）

Li Xuecong (L) and Ma Fugui of the Nu ethnic minority overlook a valley in Tuoping Village, Fugong County, Yunnan Province, Nov. 25, 2016. (Xinhua/Hu Chao)

红瑶传统中有"狗不耕田，女不读书"的观念，适龄女童一度入学率极低。广西融水苗族自治县白云乡中心校红瑶女童班于 1988 年创办，实行寄宿制且免收一切费用，有效提高了红瑶女童的入学率和巩固率。图为 2017 年 11 月 29 日拍摄的该班各族女童。（新华社记者黄孝邦摄）

The enrollment rate of school-age girls used to remain extremely low among Yao people due to their old customs. A free boarding class for girls of the ethnic group was founded in 1988 in a school in Baiyun Township, Rongshui Miao Autonomous County, Guangxi Zhuang Autonomous Region. The class greatly improves the enrollment rate of Yao girls in the region. Girls of different ethnic groups are in the class, Nov. 29, 2017. (Xinhua/Huang Xiaobang)

2017 年 9 月 6 日，在贵州省凯里市易地扶贫搬迁后新建开园的开怀街道第十三幼儿园，新入园的 4 岁苗族小女孩潘承玥在吃免费"营养午餐"。（新华社发　吴吉斌摄）

Four-year-old Pan Chengyue of the Miao ethnic group, a new student, enjoys her free lunch in the 13th kindergarten newly built as part of a relocation program for poverty relief in Kaihuai Street, Kaili City, Guizhou Province, Sept. 6, 2017. (Xinhua/Wu Jibin)

　　2017年9月3日，在广西大化瑶族自治县板升乡弄雷村哈宝屯，12岁的蒙文超（左）和小伙伴们躺在楼顶。2015年，他家从不通公路的深山搬到公路边，告别危旧的木瓦房，住进了三层小楼。（新华社记者黄孝邦摄）

Meng Wenchao (L), 12, and his friends lie on the roof of a house in Nonglei Village, Dahua Yao Autonomous County, Guangxi Zhuang Autonomous Region, Sept. 3, 2017. In 2015, his family bid farewell to a dilapidated wooden tile-roofed house in deep mountains and moved into a three-story building. (Xinhua/ Huang Xiaobang)

2017 年 6 月 15 日，广西融水苗族自治县大年乡吉格村苗族妇女袁世兰（左）、韦培税在展示苗绣。吉格村将苗绣产业作为一种重要的脱贫产业来经营，目前村里的苗绣制作已经由原来的手工发展为工厂机器织造。（新华社记者黄孝邦摄）

Yuan Shilan (L) and Wei Peishui, villagers of the Miao ethnic group, present the Miao embroidery works in Jige Village, Rongshui Miao Autonomous County, Guangxi Zhuang Autonomous Region, June 15, 2017. The embroideries are produced by machines in the factory instead of by handcrafting. (Xinhua/ Huang Xiaobang)

2018 年 2 月 13 日，云南省禄劝彝族苗族自治县中屏镇火本村小组，77 岁的李桂芳老人听到孩子就要到家的消息，露出欣喜的笑容。（新华社记者杨宗友摄）

Li Guifang, 77, wears a bright smile after hearing the news that her children come back home, in Huoben Village, Luquan Yi and Miao Autonomous County, Yunnan Province, Feb. 13, 2018. (Xinhua/Yang Zongyou)

2018 年 2 月 11 日，西藏聂荣县帕玉村玩智能手机的藏族牧女。（新华社记者觉果摄）

A Tibetan herdswoman uses her cell phone in Payu Village, Nyainrong County, Tibet Autonomous Region, Feb. 11, 2018. (Xinhua/Jogod)

2017 年 9 月 22 日，在湖南省花垣县双龙镇十八洞村，村民龙德成（左三）邀请直播团队品尝当地特产猕猴桃果汁饮料。（新华社记者王天聪摄）

Long Decheng (L 3rd) invites a livestreaming team to drink juice made of kiwi fruits in Shibadong Village, Huayuan County, central China's Hunan Province, Sept. 22, 2017. (Xinhua/Wang Tiancong)

2018 年 9 月 23 日，人们在贵州省岑巩县水尾镇马家寨村举办的庆祝活动上跳花灯。当日，当地农民举行跳花灯、舞金钱棍、展傩戏傩技等民俗表演，欢度首届中国农民丰收节。（新华社记者杨文斌摄）

Dancing with lanterns is held in Majiazhai Village, Cengong County, Guizhou Province, Sept. 23, 2018. On the day, villagers put on performances to celebrate the first Chinese Farmers' Harvest Festival. (Xinhua/Yang Wenbin)

2017 年 2 月 27 日，在广西东兰县巴畴乡巴英村，当地少数民族同胞在非物质文化遗产展演中表演，共同祈求新一年风调雨顺、五谷丰登。（新华社记者陆波岸摄）

Villagers of local ethnic groups give a performance during an intangible cultural heritage exhibition to pray for a good harvest in Baying Village, Donglan County, Guangxi Zhuang Autonomous Region, Feb. 27, 2017. (Xinhua/Lu Boan)

2018 年 2 月 8 日，陕西省延川县文安驿镇梁家河村村民在排练秧歌。（新华社发　张博文摄）

Villagers have a rehearsal of Yangko dance in Liangjiahe Village, Yanchuan County, Shaanxi Province, Feb. 8, 2018. (Xinhua/Zhang Bowen)

2018 年 7 月 18 日，贵州省六盘水市六枝特区月亮河畔，布依族群众载歌载舞庆祝传统民族节日"六月六"。（新华社记者陶亮摄）

Villagers of the Buyi ethnic group dance and sing to celebrate their traditional festival on the sixth day of the sixth lunar month along a river in Liupanshui City, Guizhou Province, July 18, 2018. (Xinhua/Tao Liang)

2019年4月17日，内蒙古兴安盟科尔沁右翼中旗巴彦敖包嘎查的村民在跳安代舞。（新华社记者彭源摄）

Drones capture the images of villagers dancing in Hinggan League of Inner Mongolia Autonomous Region, April 17, 2019. (Xinhua/Peng Yuan)

2019年2月19日，山西省武乡县大有乡王庄沟村村民在表演快板。该村在2018年年底实现整村脱贫。（新华社记者詹彦摄）

Villagers play kuaiban, a form of oral storytelling performance, in Wangzhuanggou Village, Wuxiang County, Shanxi Province, Feb. 19, 2019. The village casts off poverty at the end of 2018. (Xinhua/Zhan Yan)

2018 年 2 月 6 日，在广西南丹县八圩瑶族乡瑶寨移民安置点，白裤瑶胞敲响铜鼓。（新华社记者周华摄）

Ethnic Yao people play copper drums at a relocation point in Nandan County, south China's Guangxi Zhuang Autonomous Region, Feb. 6, 2018. (Xinhua/Zhou Hua)

2017 年 7 月 28 日，江西省会昌县文武坝镇古坊村村民在收获早稻。（新华社记者彭昭之摄）

Farmers harvest early rice in Gufang Village, Huichang County, Jiangxi Province, July 28, 2017. (Xinhua/Peng Zhaozhi)

2017 年 3 月，兰考成为河南省首个"摘帽"的贫困县。图为 2018 年 11 月 12 日拍摄的葡萄架乡黄砦村村民展示温室中的葡萄。（新华社记者冯大鹏摄）

Lankao County became Henan Province's first impoverished county that shook off poverty in March 2017. A villager from Huangzhai Village, Putaojia Township, shows his grapes in a greenhouse, Nov. 12, 2018. (Xinhua/Feng Dapeng)

2018 年 9 月 4 日，西藏日喀则市桑珠孜区东嘎乡祺玛党庆现代农业发展专业合作社社员将收获的土豆背向地头。（新华社记者张汝锋摄）

A farmer of a modern agriculture development cooperative carries potatoes in Dongkar Township, Shigatse City, Tibet Autonomous Region, Sept. 4, 2018. (Xinhua/Zhang Rufeng)

　　2018年2月4日，在湖南省花垣县十八洞村，新郎的迎亲队伍遇上新娘亲友拦门。两对分别来自湘西和湘潭的新人特地赶到十八洞村体验苗族婚礼。（新华社发　薛宇舸摄）

Groomsmen meet bridesmaids in Shibadong Village, Huayuan County, Hunan Province, Feb. 4, 2018. Two pairs of newlyweds from different parts of the province come to the village to experience its wedding tradition. (Xinhua/Xue Yuge)

奇奇里村是位于山西省永和县黄河乾坤湾对岸山崖上的一个贫困村。2015 年开始精准扶贫，至 2017 年年底，奇奇里村实现整村脱贫。图为 2018 年 2 月 23 日，冯文忠和刘翠翠举行婚礼。（新华社记者詹彦摄）

Qiqili is an impoverished village located on a cliff across the Qiankunwan river bend along the Yellow River in Yonghe County, north China's Shanxi Province. The targeted poverty alleviation for the village begins in 2015, and the whole village shakes off poverty at the end of 2017. The photo shows that Feng Wenzhong and Liu Cuicui hold their wedding ceremony on Feb. 23, 2018. (Xinhua/Zhan Yan)

2019 年 10 月 15 日，来自陕西省洛南县灵口敬老院的张金水夫妇（左）、杨红山夫妇（右）在婚姻登记现场合影留念。洛南县在脱贫攻坚工作中，对全县愿意到敬老院的 369 位五保户实行"特困集中供养"政策。（新华社记者陶明摄）

Two couples from Lingkou Nursing Home in Luonan County of Shaanxi Province take a group photo at the marriage registration site on Oct. 15, 2019. In doing poverty alleviation work, Luonan County has implemented the policy of "concentrated support for the poor" for 369 people who live on the "five guarantees" (senior or disabled people unable to work and without a source of income are guaranteed food, clothing, medical care, housing and burial expenses) and who are willing to go to the nursing home. (Xinhua/Tao Ming)

2017 年 9 月 22 日，广西融水苗族自治县香粉乡雨梅村 40 岁的陈妹琼在稻田里展示禾花鱼。最近两年，当地政府发展稻田禾花鲤鱼养殖，增加农民收入。再加上雨梅村基础设施不断完善，群众的生产生活成本极大降低，长期在家务农的陈妹琼一家于 2016 年脱贫。（新华社记者王婧嫱摄）

Chen Meiqiong, 40, from Yumei Village, Rongshui Miao Autonomous County, south China's Guangxi Zhuang Autonomous Region, shows lotus fish in a rice field on Sep. 22, 2017. In the past two years, the local government develops the cultivation of carp in rice fields to increase farmers' income. With the continuous development of the infrastructure in Yumei Village, the costs of production and living for locals are greatly reduced. Chen's family, which has been farming for a long time, is lifted out of poverty in 2016. (Xinhua/Wang Jingqiang)

2017 年 9 月 21 日，广西三江侗族自治县同乐苗族乡高岜村苗族女村医杨思在行医途中。杨思从事村医工作 16 年，以前她经常要翻山越岭去给群众看病，随着脱贫攻坚工作的深入推进，村里修了很多路，卫生室的条件也大为改观，村医的工作也轻松了不少。（新华社记者王婧嫱摄）

Yang Si, a female village doctor from the Miao ethnic group in Gaoba Village, Sanjiang Dong Autonomous County, south China's Guangxi Zhuang Autonomous Region, is on her way to visit patients on Sept. 21, 2017. Yang has been working as a village doctor for 16 years. In the past, she had to climb mountains to visit her patients. With the advancement of poverty alleviation work, roads are built in the village, and the conditions in the clinic are improved. The job of village doctors becomes much easier. (Xinhua/Wang Jingqiang)

　　2017年11月21日广西隆林各族自治县天生桥库区移民的网箱养殖户。20世纪90年代，天生桥水电站高坝蓄水后，土地被淹没的库区移民，在当地党委政府的引导下，发展水上养殖产业，逐渐脱贫致富。（新华社记者李鑫摄）

Fish farmers relocated from Tianshengqiao Reservoir area in the Longlin County, south China's Guangxi Zhuang Autonomous Region on Nov. 21, 2017. In the 1990s, after the Tianshengqiao Hydropower Station dam stores water, the displaced people in the reservoir area whose lands are flooded have developed the aquaculture industry under the guidance of the local government, and gradually get rid of poverty. (Xinhua/Li Xin)

2019 年 6 月在山西省长治市拍摄的部分生于 1949 年的老人肖像。这些共和国的同龄人亲历了长治山乡的巨变，见证着长治山区脱贫攻坚伟大工程的一步步推进。

第一排从左至右：郭耀威、尚彩良、曹晋忠、郭中其、李增福、王巨才。

第二排从左至右：崔国平、申爱苗、董留照、郑引兰、田何英、魏连保。

第三排从左至右：郝春香、魏焕英、崔翠香、王月兰、张桂香、高拉英。

第四排从左至右：申全明、牛庆山、赵树江、张元庆、史天恩、王润年。

第五排从左至右：王秀娥、王秀英、桑改风、张成华、李小俊、刘中秀。

（新华社记者詹彦、曹阳、杨晨光摄）

The photos taken in June 2019 in Changzhi City, north China's Shanxi Province show some seniors who are born in 1949. The elderly of the same age as the People's Republic of China have witnessed the huge changes and the step-by-step advancement of the great poverty alleviation project in Changzhi's mountainous areas.

The first row (from L to R): Guo Yaowei, Shang Cailiang, Cao Jinzhong, Guo Zhongqi, Li Zengfu, and Wang Jucai.

The second row (from L to R): Cui Guoping, Shen Aimiao, Dong Liuzhao, Zheng Yinlan, Tian Heying, and Wei Lianbao.

The third row (from L to R): Hao Chunxiang, Wei Huanying, Cui Cuixiang, Wang Yuelan, Zhang Guixiang, and Gao Laying.

The fourth row (from L to R): Shen Quanming, Niu Qingshan, Zhao Shujiang, Zhang Yuanqing, Shi Tianen, and Wang Runnian.

The fifth row (from L to R): Wang Xiu'e, Wang Xiuying, Sang Gaifeng, Zhang Chenghua, Li Xiaojun, and Liu Zhongxiu. (Xinhua/Zhan Yan, Cao Yang, Yang Chenguang)

2019 年 1 月 3 日，甘肃省徽县嘉陵镇稻坪村入股徽县青泥岭树蜜稻坪农民专业合作社经营蜂业的 79 户村民，现场领取了共计 46 万多元的个人与集体分红。（新华社记者陈斌摄）

A total of 79 households in Daoping Village, Huixian County, northwest China's Gansu Province receive more than 460,000 yuan in individual and collective dividends for taking a stake in the apiculture of a farmers' cooperative in the county on Jan. 3, 2019. (Xinhua/Chen Bin)

2019 年 5 月 21 日，培训合格的农民在陕西省三原县陵前镇领到新型职业农民证书。近年来，三原县开展形式多样的新型职业农民技能培训工作，目前已有 1173 人获得证书，创办专业合作社和家庭农场 128 个。（新华社记者刘潇摄）

Trained farmers receive certificates for new-type professional farmers in Lingqian Township, Sanyuan County, northwest China's Shaanxi Province on May 21, 2019. In recent years, Sanyuan County has carried out various forms of skill training for new-type farmers. A total of 1,173 people have obtained certificates and 128 cooperatives and family farms have been established. (Xinhua/Liu Xiao)

2019 年 11 月 18 日，在河北省邢台县晏家屯镇心长村扶贫小院里，村民在晾晒、整理手工饰品。（新华社记者牟宇摄）

Villagers dry and sort handmade ornaments in a "poverty alleviation courtyard" in Xinchang Village, Yanjiatun Township, Xingtai County, north China's Hebei Province on Nov. 18, 2019. The township implements the project of "poverty alleviation courtyard" in combination with the poverty alleviation work and the needs of the impoverished villagers. The project helps more than 200 people increase income through handicraft production, flower planting and other methods. (Xinhua/Mou Yu)

　　2019 年 4 月 19 日，西藏拉萨市尼木县民间艺术团演员在卡如乡卡如村二组的村广场上排练节目，为即将到来的旅游旺季做准备。（新华社记者晋美多吉摄）

Performers from a folk art troupe of Nimu County, Lhasa City, southwest China's Tibet Autonomous Region rehearse in a village square to prepare for the upcoming tourist season on April 19, 2019. (Xinhua/Jigme Dorje)

2019年8月9日，西藏当雄县举行竞争激烈的民间传统拔河比赛。（新华社记者刘洁摄）

A traditional tug-of-war competition is held in Damxung County, Tibet Autonomous Region on Aug. 9, 2019. (Xinhua/Liu Jie)

2019年9月6日，演员在2019·西藏"中国农民丰收节"暨扎囊氆氇文化节开幕式上再现青稞丰收场景。（新华社记者张汝锋摄）

Actors perform the highland barley harvest scene at the opening ceremony marking the 2019 Chinese farmers harvest festival in Tibet on Sept. 6, 2019. (Xinhua/Zhang Rufeng)

　　2020 年 6 月 24 日，绣娘在青海省互助土族自治县举办的端午节香包"选美"大赛上交流。（新华社记者解统强摄）

Female embroiderers exchange views at a sachet competition during the Dragon Boat Festival in Huzhu Tu Autonomous County, northwest China's Qinghai Province on June 24, 2020. (Xinhua/Xie Tongqiang)

　　2020 年 6 月 25 日，演员在新疆塔什库尔干塔吉克自治县端午节群众性文化体育活动现场表演。（新华社记者胡虎虎摄）

Actors perform at a mass cultural and sports event during the Dragon Boat Festival in Tashkurgan Tajik Autonomous County, northwest China's Xinjiang Uygur Autonomous Region on June 25, 2020. (Xinhua/Hu Huhu)

　　2019 年 11 月 18 日，在广西柳州市融水苗族自治县易地扶贫安置点苗家小镇"妇女之家巾帼扶贫车间"，妇女们在学习刺绣。（新华社记者黄孝邦摄）

Women learn embroidery at a resettlement site for poverty alleviation in Rongshui Miao Autonomous County, Liuzhou City, south China's Guangxi Zhuang Autonomous Region on Nov. 18, 2019. (Xinhua/Huang Xiaobang)

2020 年 10 月 17 日，在湖南省永州市道县梅花镇贵头村，带货主播通过网络直播销售葡萄。当日是第 7 个国家扶贫日，多地举行形式多样的消费扶贫活动，展示扶贫成效，助力脱贫攻坚。（新华社发　何红福摄）

Live-streamers sell grapes online in Guitou Village, Daoxian County, central China's Hunan Province, Oct. 17, 2020. On the seventh National Poverty Alleviation Day, various forms of poverty alleviation through consumption are held in many places in China. (Xinhua/He Hongfu)

2019 年 10 月 17 日，在江西省南昌市南昌县八一乡南江村，工作人员把招聘岗位信息发放到村民手中。当日是第 6 个国家扶贫日，江西省南昌市南昌县八一乡在南江村开展"农闲送岗家门口"主题活动，发布乡镇及周边企业的 58 个岗位招聘信息供农户选择。同时，活动还邀请当地的脱贫典型为村民进行宣讲，介绍脱贫经验。（新华社记者彭昭之摄）

Local staff distribute job vacancy handouts to villagers in Nanjiang Village, Nanchang County, east China's Jiangxi Province, Oct. 17, 2019. On the sixth National Poverty Alleviation Day, farmers in Nanjiang Village were offered 58 job opportunities in the township and neighboring enterprises. (Xinhua/Peng Zhaozhi)

2019 年 10 月 17 日，在江西省吉安市新干县沂江乡开展的贫困户农特产品定购会上，贫困户刘秋桂（右二）向购买者介绍他养殖的泥鳅。当日是第 6 个国家扶贫日，江西省新干县各乡镇组织扶贫日主题活动。（新华社记者冯为民摄）

Liu Qiugui (second from right), who is registered as living below the poverty line, introduces his farmed loach to buyers at a trade event for special agricultural products in Xin'gan County, east China's Jiangxi Province, Oct. 17, 2019. (Xinhua/Feng Weimin)

2017 年 10 月 17 日，福建省宁德市古田县纪委结对帮扶干部苏东北（右一）在向县城东街道桃溪村脱贫户游良进夫妇（左一、左二）了解扶贫小额信贷资金的使用情况。当日是第 4 个国家扶贫日。福建省宁德市古田县组织扶贫办、纪检监察等相关单位的工作人员前往各自联系结对的精准扶贫对象家中进行入户回访，与他们商讨发展措施，帮助他们解决生产发展资金难题。2016 年，古田县成立扶贫小额信贷促进会，并设 1417 万元"扶贫小额信贷风险资金池"，有效解决贫困户创业的资金难题。（新华社记者魏培全摄）

Su Dongbei (first from right), an official of the discipline inspection commission of Gutian County, east China's Fujian Province, learns about the use of micro-credit funds for poverty alleviation from a poverty-stricken couple, Oct. 17, 2017. In 2016, Gutian county set up a poverty alleviation micro-finance promotion association with a capital pool of 14.17 million yuan, to solve the capital shortage problem which poor households have in business startups. (Xinhua/Wei Peiquan)

从柬埔寨首都金边向北驱车约一个小时就到了干丹省莫穆坎普县斯瓦安普乡。澜湄合作早期收获项目阶段性成果之———中国援柬减贫示范合作项目推动这里的两个扶贫村在新冠疫情下持续发展，焕发出新活力。图为 2020 年 8 月 17 日在柬埔寨干丹省莫穆坎普县斯瓦安普乡拍摄的中国援柬减贫示范合作项目建设的水塔。（新华社发）

About an hour's drive from Phnom Penh, capital of Cambodia, is Svay Ampea commune, Kandal province. As one of the initial outcomes of the Lancang-Mekong Cooperation projects, the China-assisted poverty alleviation demonstration and cooperation project in Cambodia has promoted the sustained development of the two poverty-stricken villages. Photo taken on Aug. 17, 2020 shows the water tower built under the program. (Xinhua)

老挝南塔河 1 号水电站是中国南方电网公司在"一带一路"倡议下开发的第一个境外 BOT（建设—经营—转让）水电项目，为当地经济发展提供了保障。电站让这里的山区通电、通路，有利于村民发展生产。图为 2019 年 3 月 20 日，从库区看到的老挝南塔河 1 号水电站。（新华社记者王婧嫱摄）

A picture of the Nam Tha River 1 Hydropower Plant in Laos taken on March 20, 2019. The plant is the first overseas BOT (build-operation-transfer) hydroelectric project carried out by China Southern Power Grid under the framework of the Belt and Road Initiative. The project provides a guarantee for local economic development, with the mountainous areas having access to electricity and roads. (Xinhua/Wang Jingqiang)

中国援老挝减贫示范合作技术援助项目在万象市版索村和琅勃拉邦省象龙村开展。自2017年9月30日启动至今，两个示范项目村基础设施建设和公共服务改善项目取得显著成效，生计发展项目基本完成实施，能力建设活动持续开展。上图为2020年9月15日在老挝万象市版索村拍摄的远处的老木桥和近处中国援建的桥梁。下图为2020年9月15日在老挝万象市版索村拍摄的老木桥。（新华社发 凯乔摄）

Since its launch on Sept. 30, 2017, the China-aided Laos Poverty Reduction Demonstration Cooperation Technical Assistance project, has been carried out in Ban Xor village in Vientiane City, and another village in Luang Prabang to apply China's experience in shaking off poverty. The picture above shows the new bridge in Ban Xor village, built with aid from China; and the picture below shows the old wooden bridge, Sept. 15, 2020. (Photo by Kaikeo Saiyasane/ Xinhua)

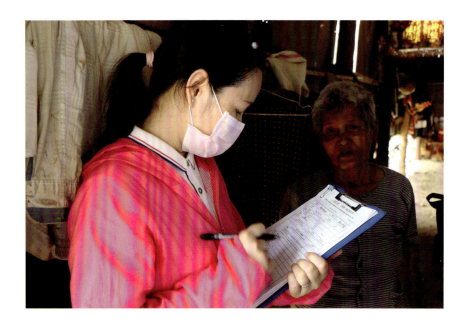

2020 年 5 月 15 日，在柬埔寨干丹省莫穆坎普县的斯瓦安普乡，中国援助柬埔寨减贫示范合作项目中方专家组柬文翻译周冰姣（左）与村民交谈。（新华社发　高炳南摄）

Zhou Bingjiao (left), member of the Chinese expert team aiding Cambodia's poverty reduction, talks with villagers in Muk Kampol district's Svay Ampea commune，Kandal province, May 15, 2020. (Xinhua/Gao Bingnan)

　　2015 年，为推进"一带一路"建设和对外减贫合作，中国国际扶贫中心和广西外资扶贫项目管理中心委托广西农业职业技术学院，依托该院在老挝承建的中国—老挝合作农作物优良品种试验站开展中老合作社区减贫示范项目建设。图为 2019 年 2 月 28 日在老挝首都万象北部的金花村拍摄的中国—老挝减贫合作社区示范项目有机蔬菜种植区。（新华社记者章建华摄）

Photo taken on Feb. 28, 2019 shows the organic vegetable growing area of the community demonstration project under the China-Laos poverty alleviation cooperation program in a village north of Vientiane. In 2015, to promote international poverty alleviation cooperation, the Guangxi Agricultural Vocational College was entrusted by the International Poverty Reduction Center in China and the foreign-funded poverty alleviation project management center of south China's Guangxi region to undertake the construction of the community demonstration project focusing on good crop varieties. (Xinhua/Zhang Jianhua)

2016 年 9 月 26 日，在肯尼亚内罗毕，一名工作人员走进中非联合研究中心。 中非联合研究中心是中非双方共同建设的首个综合性科研和教育基础设施。（新华社记者潘思危摄）

A staff member walks into the China-Africa Joint Research Center in Nairobi, Kenya, Sept. 26, 2016. The center is the first comprehensive research and education facility jointly built by China and Africa. (Xinhua/Pan Siwei)

2018 年 9 月 4 日，来自中国的农业技术指导李昌洪在肯尼亚西部的纳库鲁郡指导当地农民种植除虫菊。（新华社记者李琰摄）

Li Changhong, an agricultural technical instructor from China, instructs local farmers to plant pyrethrum in Nakuru County, western Kenya, Sept. 4, 2018. (Xinhua/Li Yan)

2020 年 8 月 21 日拍摄的云南昭通鲁甸易地扶贫搬迁安置区。（新华社记者刘大伟摄）

Photo taken on Aug. 21, 2020 shows the resettlement area in Ludian County, southwest China's Yunnan Province. (Xinhua/Liu Dawei)

2021 年 2 月 25 日，全国脱贫攻坚总结表彰大会在北京人民大会堂隆重举行。（新华社记者谢环驰摄）

A grand gathering is held to mark the nation's poverty alleviation accomplishments and honor model poverty fighters at the Great Hall of the People in Beijing, capital of China, Feb. 25, 2021. (Xinhua/Xie Huanchi)

紧密团结在以习近平同志为核心的党中央周围，全面推进乡村振兴，巩固拓展脱贫

图书在版编目(CIP)数据

决战决胜 : 中国脱贫攻坚的伟大实践 : 汉文、英文 /
新华通讯社, 原国务院扶贫开发领导小组办公室编.
——北京 : 新华出版社, 2024.1
ISBN 978-7-5166-7293-8

Ⅰ. ①决… Ⅱ. ①新… ②原… Ⅲ. ①扶贫—成就—中国—画册 Ⅳ. ①F126-64

中国国家版本馆CIP数据核字(2024)第011558号

决战决胜:中国脱贫攻坚的伟大实践

编　　者:新华通讯社　原国务院扶贫开发领导小组办公室

出 版 人:匡乐成　　　　　　　　　　　　出版统筹:许　新　黄春峰
责任编辑:徐　光　唐波勇　李　成　刘宏森　装帧设计:李尘工作室

出版发行:新华出版社
地　　址:北京石景山区京原路8号　　　　　邮　　编:100040
网　　址:http://www.xinhuapub.com
经　　销:新华书店、新华出版社天猫旗舰店、京东旗舰店及各大网店
购书热线:010—63077122　　　　　　中国新闻书店购书热线:010—63072012

照　　排:六合方圆
印　　刷:北京新华印刷有限公司

成品尺寸:240mm×305mm
印　　张:59　　　　　　　　　　　　字　　数:60千字
版　　次:2024年1月第一版　　　　　　印　　次:2024年1月第一次印刷

书　　号:ISBN 978-7-5166-7293-8
定　　价:698.00元